Quick Start Drawing

BASICS

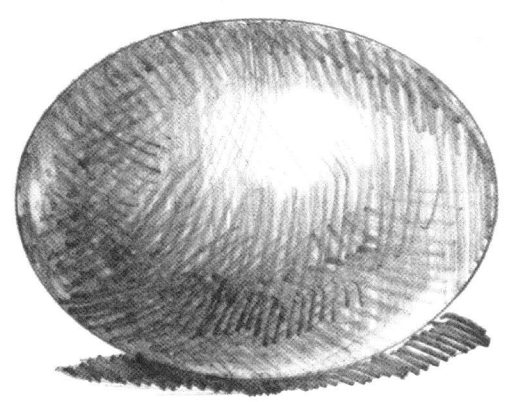

Walter Foster

About This Book

Do you want to learn to draw? Perhaps you've tried several times, but you didn't stick with it. Why not restart your drawing journey now with *Quick Start Drawing Basics*? Packed with dozens of drawing prompts, helpful techniques, simple step-by-step lessons, and easy tracing exercises, this drawing pad is ideal for beginning artists who enjoy learning by doing. As such, you will build basic art knowledge and drawing skills in a short time, while you learn to create your own unique artwork along the way.

You'll start with the basics, including learning about the tools of the trade. From there, you will discover easy techniques, including how to hold the pencil and how to draw common pencil strokes. You will continue on by learning how to draw basic shapes and develop them with shading. Finally, dozens of drawing tutorials featuring flowers, nature, animals, and people will have you practicing your skills in no time. This drawing pad is designed to be brought to life by you, so we've also included unfinished drawings printed in light gray to use as a foundation on which to master your talent. It's the perfect starting point for beginners. High-quality paper means you can draw inside without worrying about the pages underneath, so be brave and experiment! We recommend keeping a sketchbook or sketch pad in addition to this drawing pad so that you can continue to practice the featured lessons.

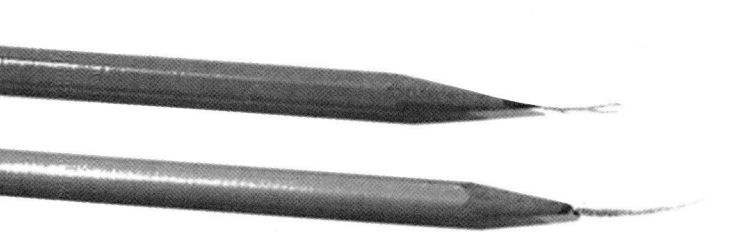

Getting Started

Drawing doesn't require a lot of materials. A good HB pencil and this pad are perfect for getting started. The next few pages go over the fundamentals of drawing, including the tools and materials, how to hold and sharpen a pencil, and how to create a variety of basic strokes. A good drawing features a lively interplay between light and dark, so you will learn a bit about shading techniques and creating a value scale. Throughout this pad, look for step-by-step projects like the one shown below to help guide you through the drawing process. Let's get started!

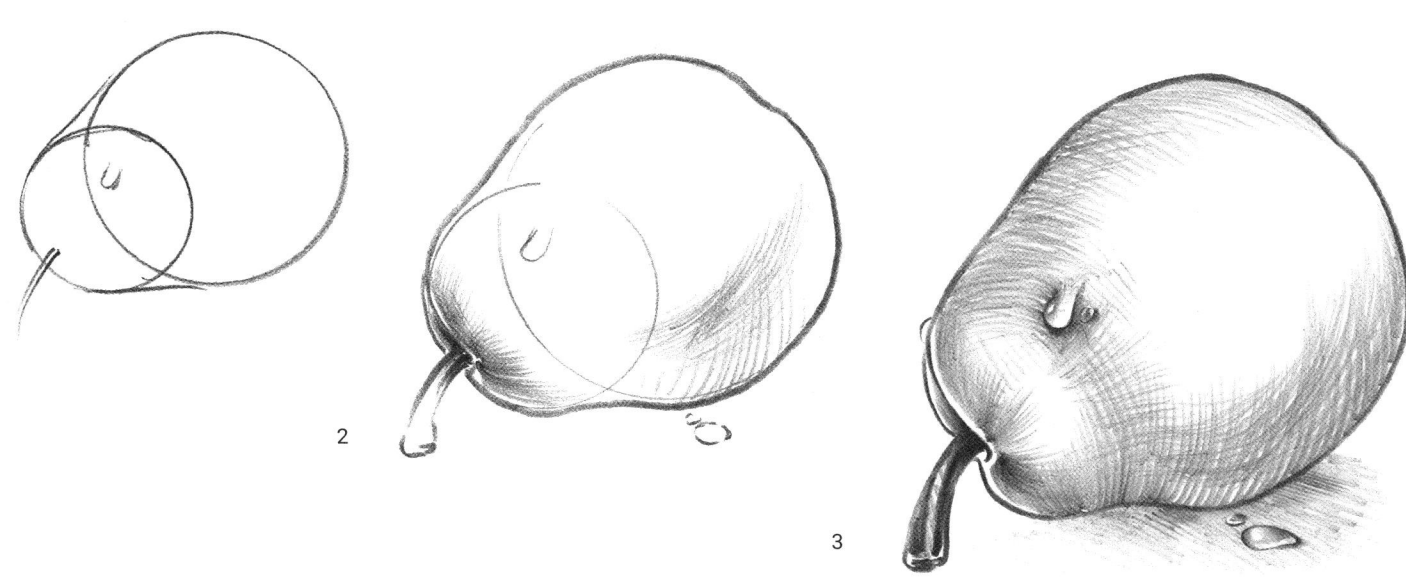

1

2

3

Tools and Materials

Pencils are classified according to the hardness of the lead. H leads are always hard. B leads are soft leads and better suited for darker lines. HB leads are in between H and B; these pencils are incredibly versatile. Start with an H pencil and an HB pencil. Make sure you have a standard pencil sharpener on hand as well as an artist's knife for more precise sharpening. You will also need erasers and extra drawing paper for practicing. As your skills improve, you can expand your artist's tool kit.

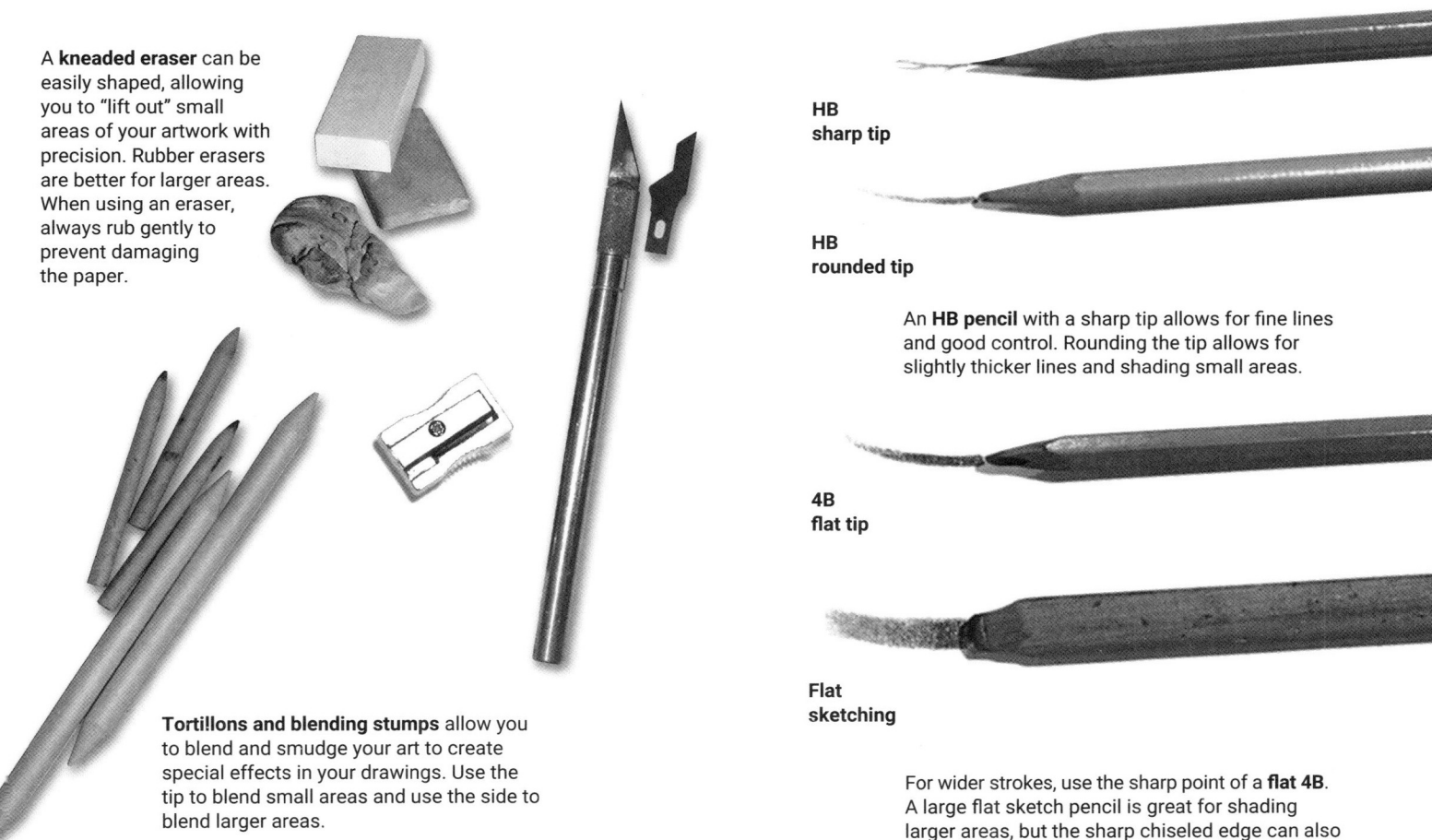

A **kneaded eraser** can be easily shaped, allowing you to "lift out" small areas of your artwork with precision. Rubber erasers are better for larger areas. When using an eraser, always rub gently to prevent damaging the paper.

Tortillons and blending stumps allow you to blend and smudge your art to create special effects in your drawings. Use the tip to blend small areas and use the side to blend larger areas.

HB sharp tip

HB rounded tip

An **HB pencil** with a sharp tip allows for fine lines and good control. Rounding the tip allows for slightly thicker lines and shading small areas.

4B flat tip

Flat sketching

For wider strokes, use the sharp point of a **flat 4B**. A large flat sketch pencil is great for shading larger areas, but the sharp chiseled edge can also be used to make thin, crisp lines.

Sharpening Pencils

There are many ways to sharpen your drawing pencils outside of using a standard handheld sharpener. Try each of the methods below to see which one you prefer.

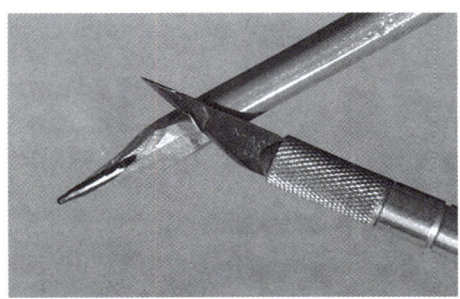

Artist knives are ideal for shaping pencils in specific ways to give them a chisel-shaped, blunt, or flat tip. Hold the knife at an angle to the pencil and carve away from the body. Always cut only a small amount of the lead and wood.

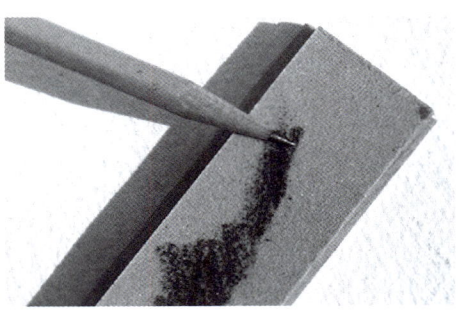

Use a **sandpaper block** to quickly shape a lead. Sandpaper also removes some of the wood coating. The finer the grit, the better you can control the result. You'll need to roll the pencil in your hand while sharpening to ensure the lead sharpens evenly.

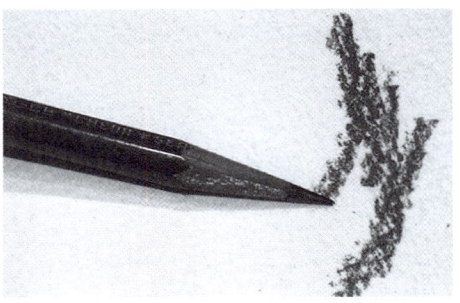

Rough paper is ideal for finely grinding a lead that you've sharpened with sandpaper. This creates a very sharp pencil for tiny, fine details. Here, too, you'll need to rotate the pencil.

Holding the Pencil

There are different ways to hold a pencil, each of which has its own purpose. When drawing, use the strength and dexterity of your entire arm to prevent your wrist and fingers from cramping or getting too tight. Try to maintain a relaxed position and hold the pencil lightly.

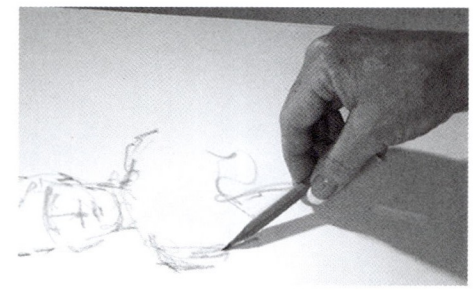

Basic Underhand This technique is suitable for creating quick scribbles on location or for shading smaller areas. You can draw bold lines of varying thickness depending on how hard you press. Although a loose grip allows you to create detailed strokes, they still appear relatively loose and free.

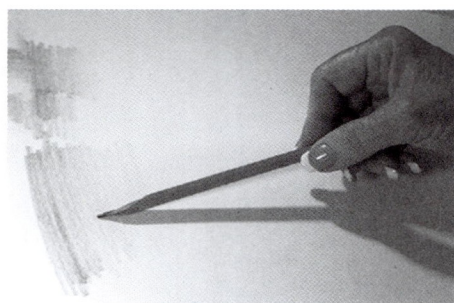

Underhand Variation When you work from the wrist, your arm and hand can move freely. This is essential for large, loose strokes. You especially need this when drawing animals from life. From the wrist, you can also draw wonderfully flat strokes, which you can use to shade larger areas, such as fur or skin. This technique is also suitable for backgrounds.

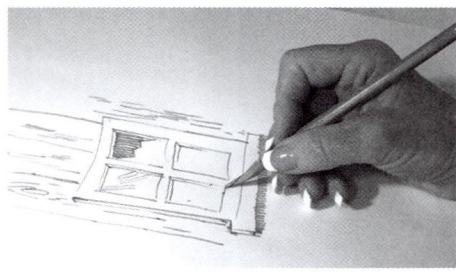

Writing Holding the pencil as you would when writing allows for the best control. This allows you to create fine, precise lines for details and accents. Place a clean sheet of paper under the heel of your hand to prevent smudging your drawing. Sharpen the pencil often to keep the lines clean and crisp.

Draw a few lines and squiggles using the three different
pencil-holding techniques. How does each grip
change your drawing?

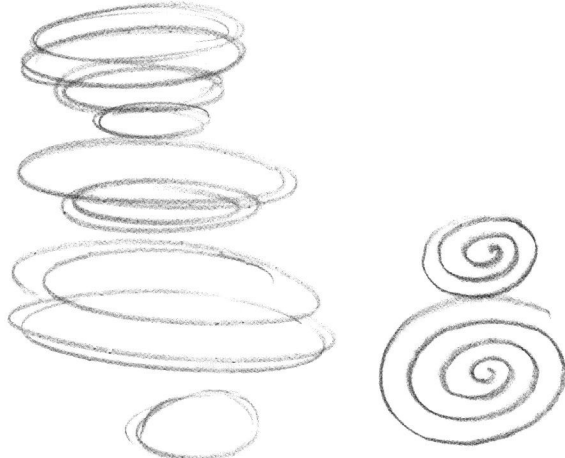

Basic Techniques

When learning to draw, it's helpful to try out a variety of drawing pencils to observe how the lines you draw change with each pencil. Finely detailed drawings are best rendered with a sharpened pencil, held in the writing position. Larger areas of a drawing are easier to shade with the flat side of a pencil held from your wrist. Be curious and try each hand position with different pencils. You'll be excited by the different results!

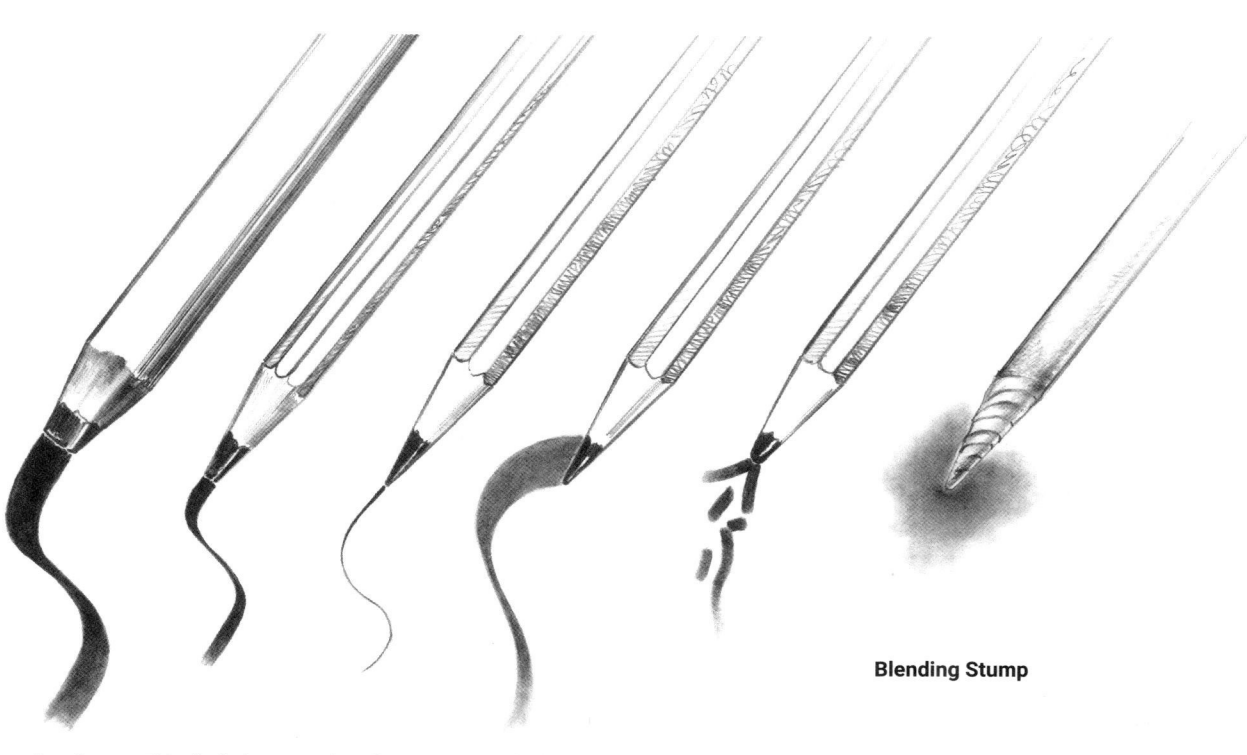

Blending Stump

Flat Tip **Chiseled Tip** **Pointed Tip** **Rounded Tip** **Blunt Tip**

Practicing basic techniques will help you understand how to manipulate the pencil to achieve a variety of effects. Practice the techniques shown below in the areas provided.

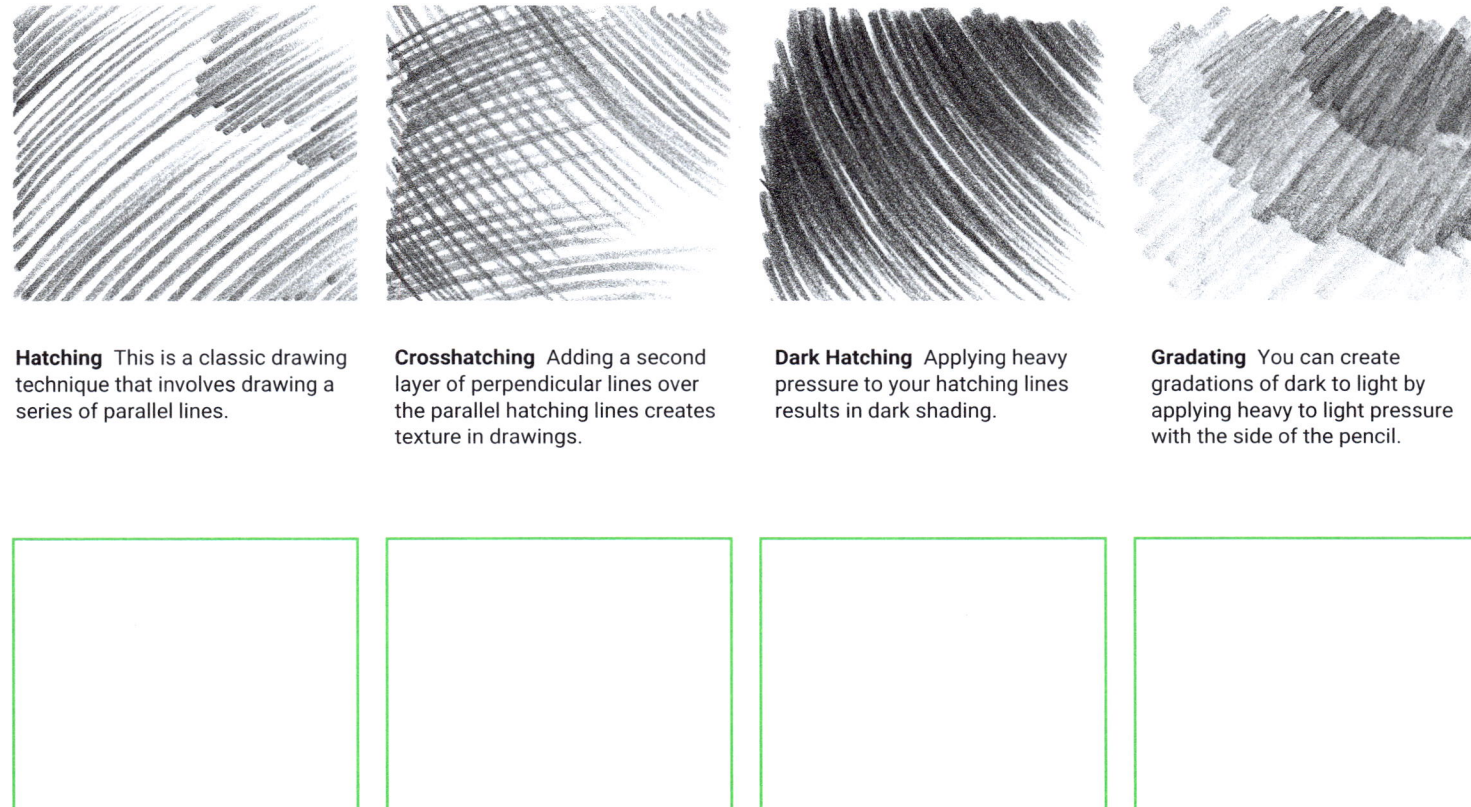

Hatching This is a classic drawing technique that involves drawing a series of parallel lines.

Crosshatching Adding a second layer of perpendicular lines over the parallel hatching lines creates texture in drawings.

Dark Hatching Applying heavy pressure to your hatching lines results in dark shading.

Gradating You can create gradations of dark to light by applying heavy to light pressure with the side of the pencil.

Seeing Values

Value is the basic term used to describe the relative lightness or darkness of a color. In pencil drawing, the values range from white to grays to black, and it's the variation among lights and darks (made with shading) and the range of values in shadows and highlights that give a two-dimensional drawing a three-dimensional look. This value scale shows the gradation from black, the darkest value, through various shades of gray and ending with white, the lightest value.

Create your own value scales in the areas below. Use an HB pencil to create one value scale. Then use pencils of varying hardness (2B, HB, and H) to create another value scale. Compare how the different pencils create different effects.

Basic Shapes

Anyone can draw just about anything by simply breaking down the subject into a few basic shapes: circles, rectangles, squares, and triangles. By drawing an outline around the basic shapes of your subject, you have drawn its shape. But your subject also has depth and dimension, or form. The corresponding forms of the basic shapes are spheres, cylinders, cubes, and cones. Sketching the shapes and developing their forms is the first step of every drawing. After that, it's essentially just connecting and refining the lines and adding details.

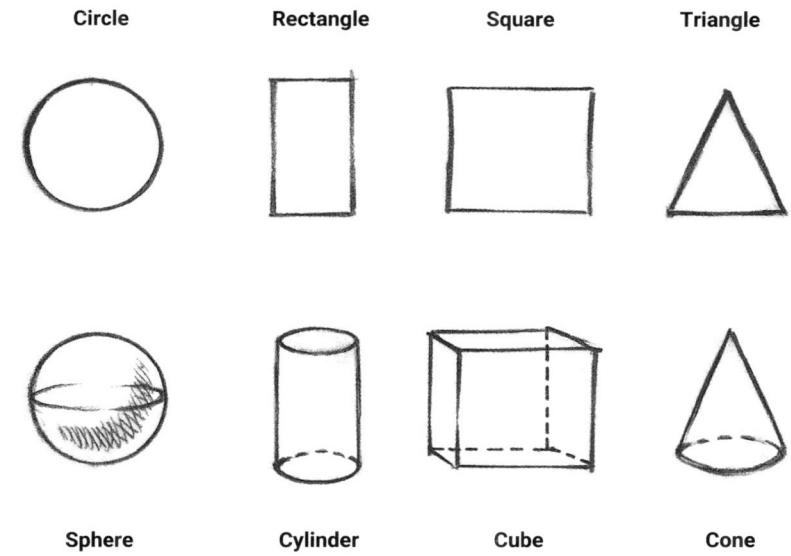

These diagrams show to how to draw the forms of these four basic shapes. The ellipses show the backs of the circle, cylinder, and cone, and the cube is drawn by connecting two squares with parallel lines.

Draw a circle, rectangle, square, and triangle.
Then create their three-dimensional forms.

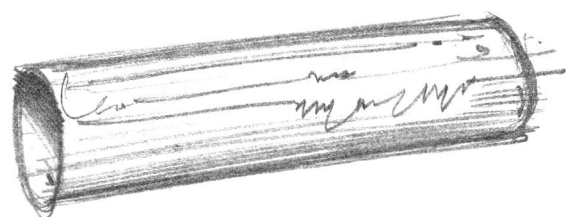

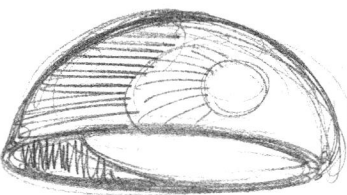

Building Forms

Once you've established the general shape and form of the subject using basic shapes, refine your drawing by applying value through hatching, crosshatching, and gradating. Gather some objects from around your home or continue to practice using basic shapes.

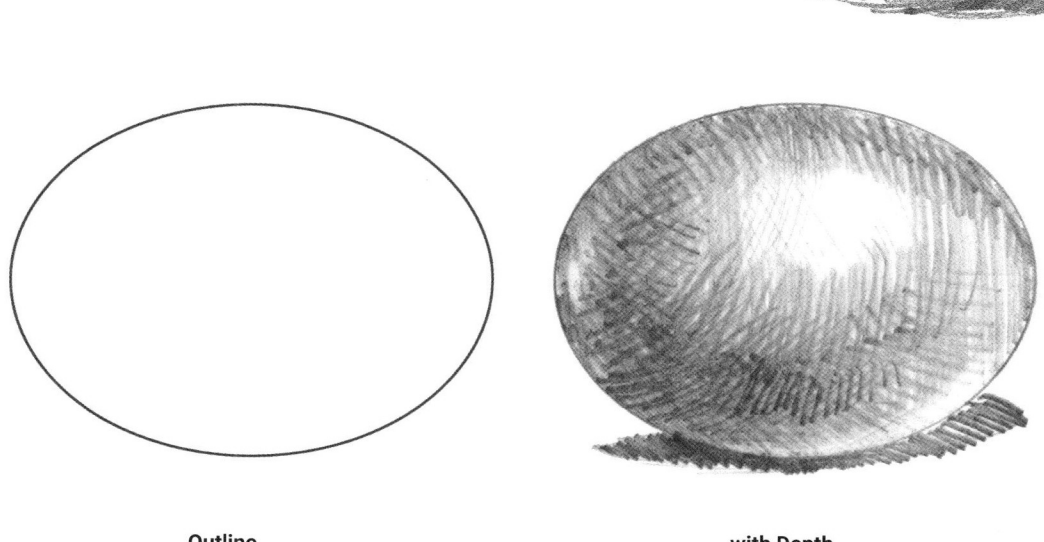

Outline   **with Depth**

The secret to transforming an outline into a form is proper shading. Use less pressure for lighter areas and more pressure for darker areas. When hatching, consider where the light is coming from. A reflection is created on the area where the light hits directly onto the object, creating the brightest area. Also consider the cast shadow, which is the shadow cast by your object. Directly above the darkest part of the cast shadow, the object is very light—like the egg shown, above right.

Develop some forms and their shadows. Try using different types of pencils, and experiment with different pressures to get a feel for them.

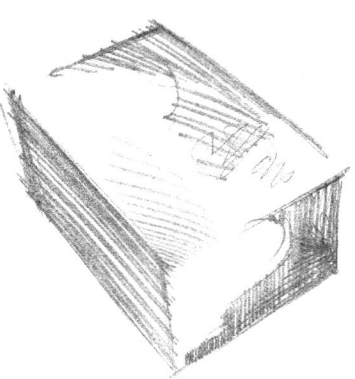

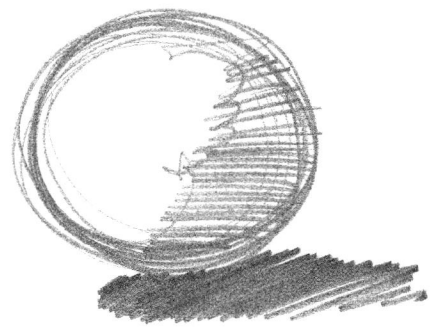

Shapes and Forms

The best way to practice drawing three-dimensional objects is to closely observe as many objects around you as possible. Look for the basic shape in each object to start. You can also arrange a simple still life, like the one below, or work from photographs and paintings. Don't be afraid to tackle more complex shapes—even the most difficult drawings start with basic shapes!

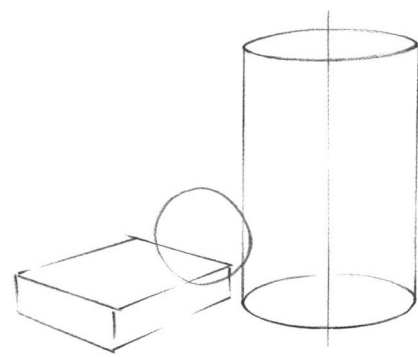

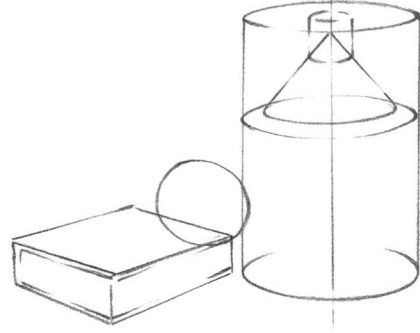

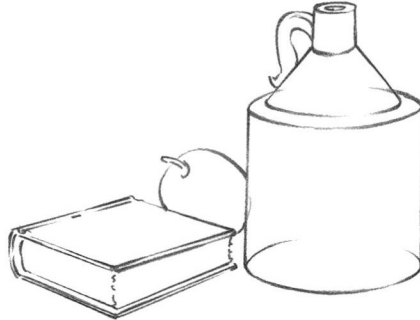

1 Begin with squares and circles for the jug and book. Add ellipses to begin building out the forms. Add a small circle to begin the apple. Notice that the whole apple shape is drawn, not just the part that will be visible. This is known as drawing ▓through."

2 Next, add ellipses for the body of the jug, a cone for the neck, and a cylinder for the spout. Pencil in a few lines on the sides of the book, parallel to the top and bottom, to begin developing its form.

3 Refine the outlines of the shapes. Once you're happy with the drawing, erase all of the sketch lines to complete your drawing.

Use the outline below to practice building out forms.
Pay attention to shading for adding light and shadows.

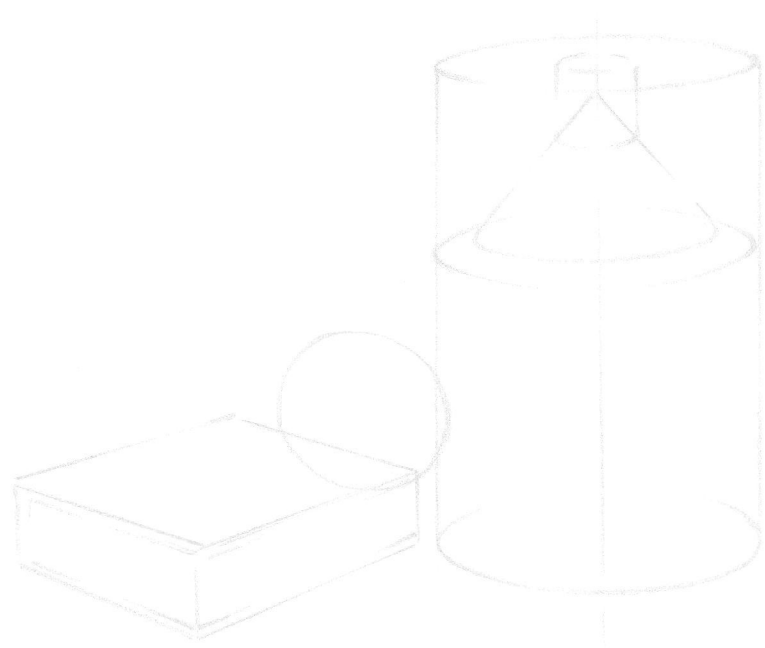

Pear

The simplest still life includes depictions of individual objects. However, fruit and vegetables are also very popular, either alone or against a natural background. Observe your subject until you are able to identify its basic shapes to draw. The pear below is created from overlapping circles: one large and one small. Add hatching to reflect its form and shape.

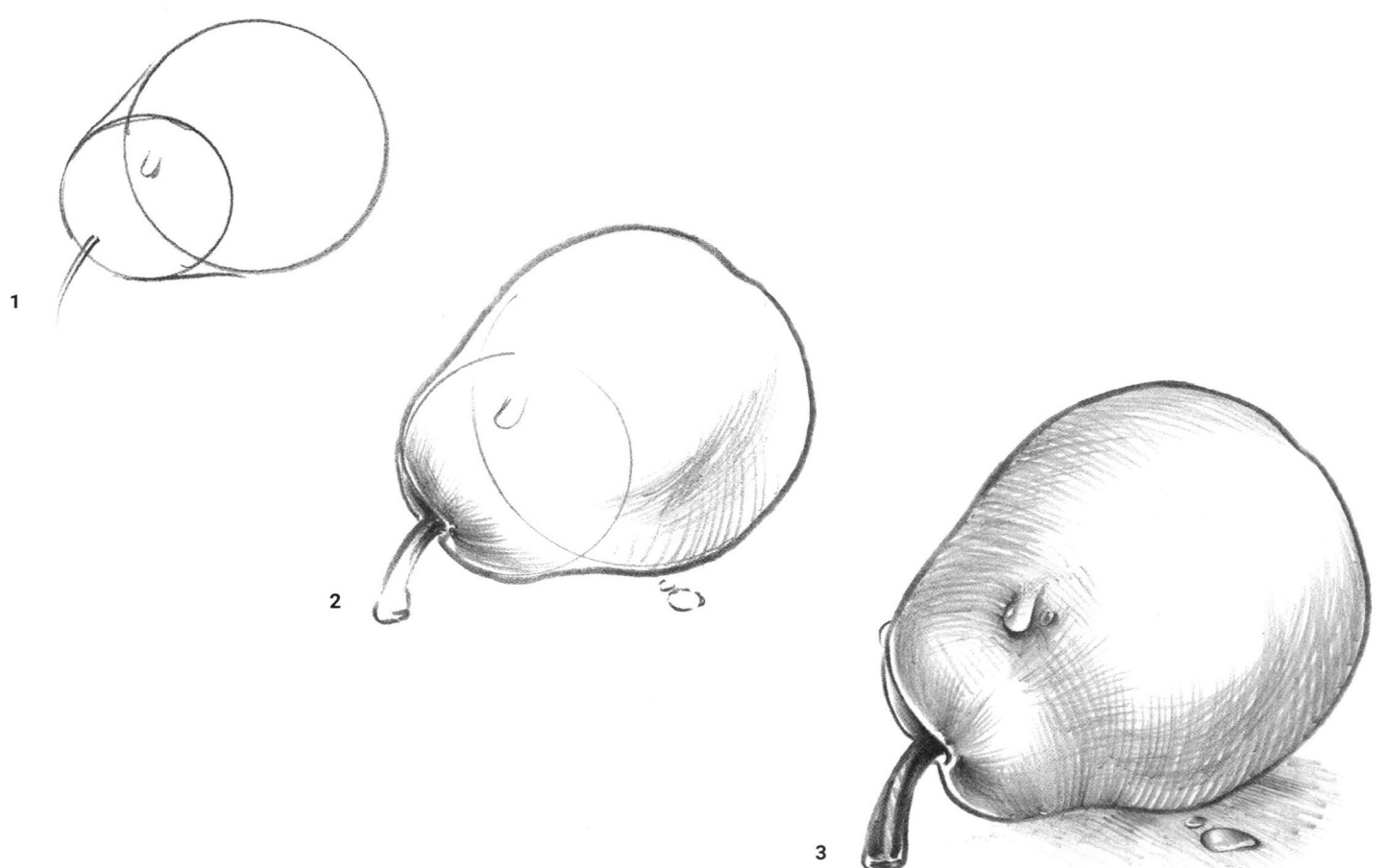

Shade the pear below with hatching to develop its form.
Make sure the hatching follows the pear's natural shape.

Peach

Start with the shapes as shown in steps one and two. Create guidelines for the pit and the peach slice. Shade the skin with longer, softer, slightly curved strokes, as shown in step three. For the dark indentations on the pit and the inside of the slice, use a 2B pencil. Finally, draw a few lines that point like rays from the pit into the flesh.

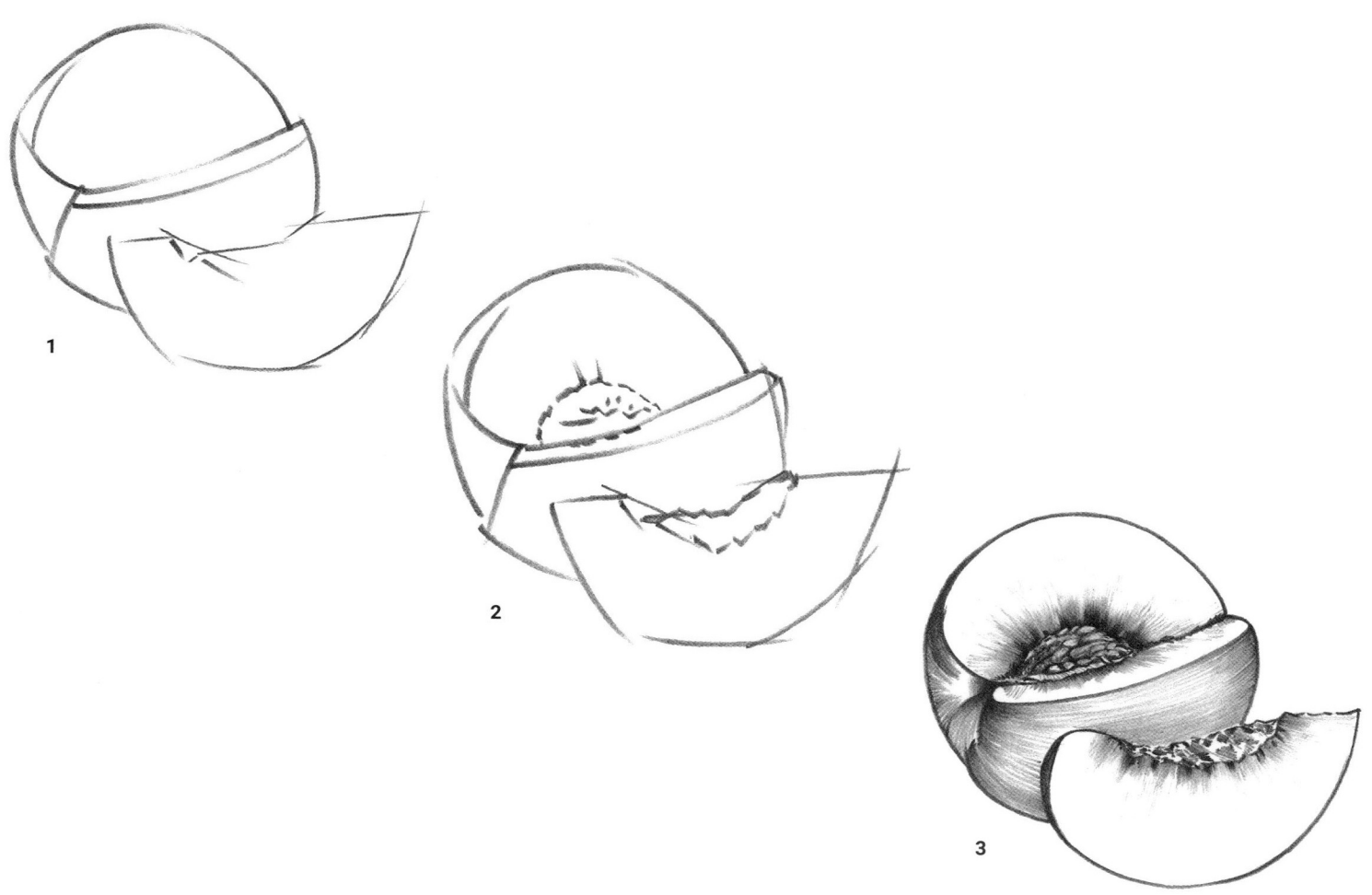

Complete the peach below by adding hatching and shading in various shades of gray.

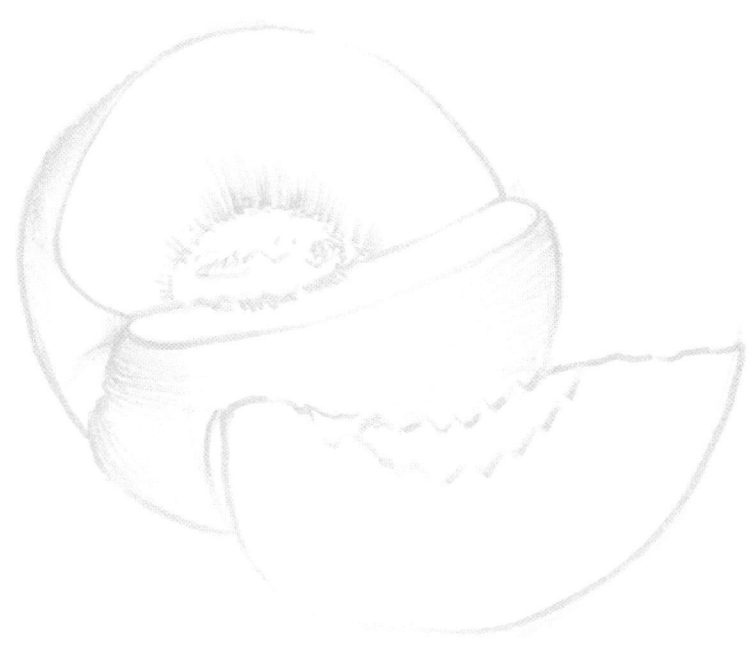

Drawing Flowers

When learning to draw flowers, it's helpful to observe your subjects closely so you can determine how to apply shading to best capture their shapes. For these simple exercises, you only need two techniques: hatching and crosshatching.

Hatching **Crosshatching**

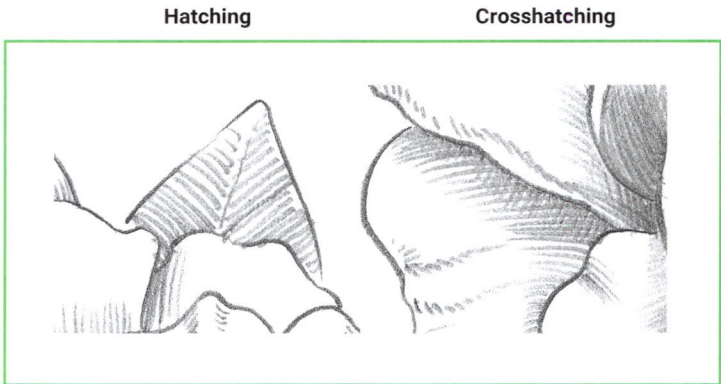

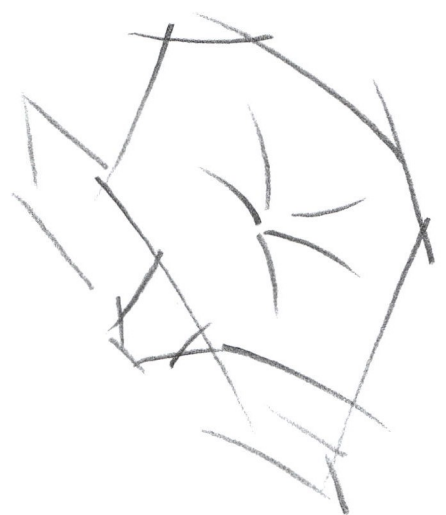

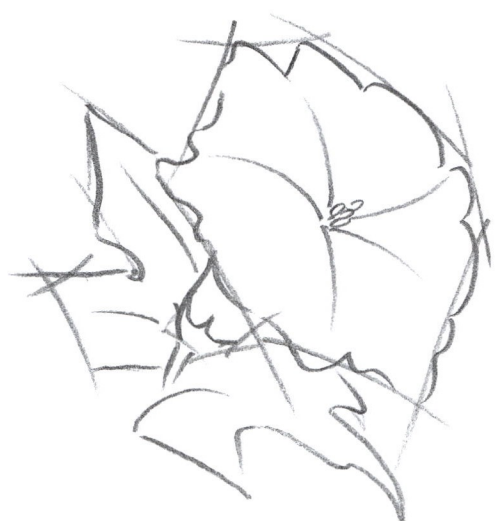

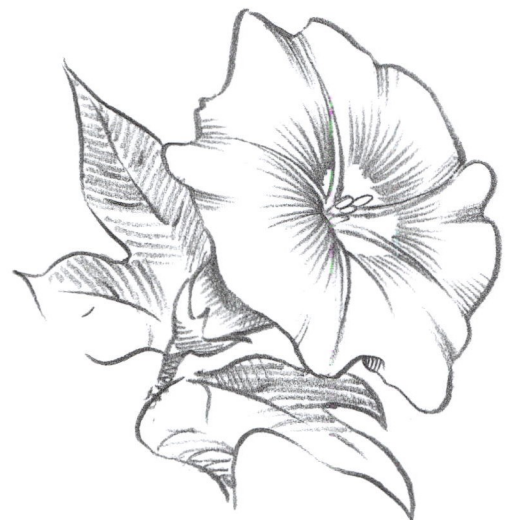

1 Take a close look at this flower. Using light strokes and a sharp HB pencil, draw a basic outline. In this three-quarter view, the petals are clearly visible. Draw the five main veins that emerge from the center of the flower. Add a few sketch lines for the leaves and stem.

2 Next, using curved lines, draw the outlines of the flower and leaves. You can adjust the thickness of the strokes and lines to your liking by applying pressure to the pencil. Finally, draw the stamens in the center.

3 Round the tip of your pencil slightly and draw clean, parallel lines that follow the shapes of the flower and leaves. With a 2B pencil, apply darker shading to areas in shadow.

Trace the outlines of the drawing below.
Apply shading to bring this flower to life.

Tulip

The harmonious flow of lines in this tulip is striking. Define the basic shape with a few lines, as shown in step one. Continue to build the form, including adding a second flower, as shown in step two. Finesse the details in step three.

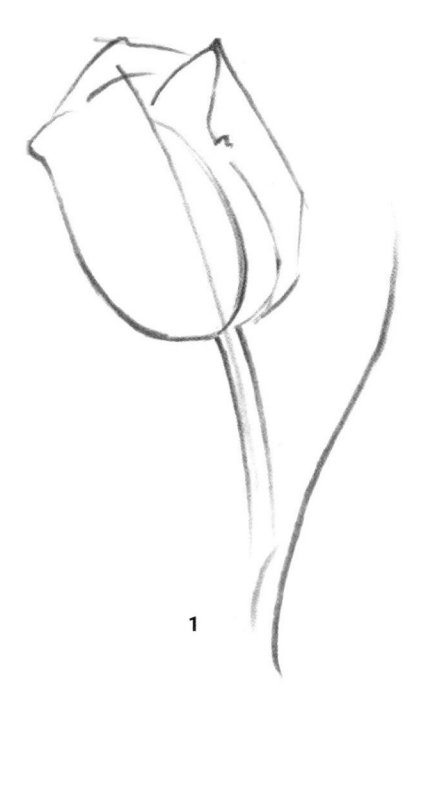

1

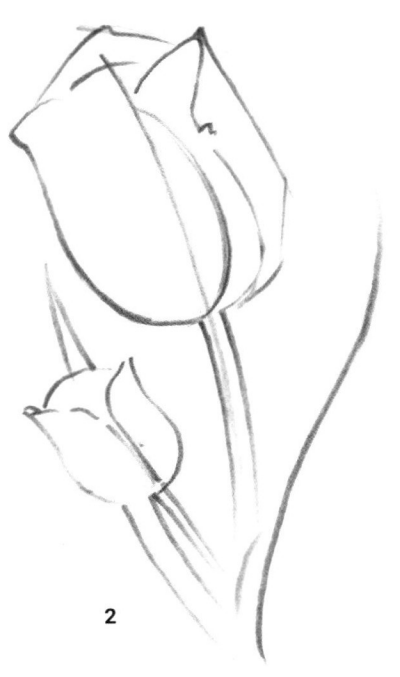

2

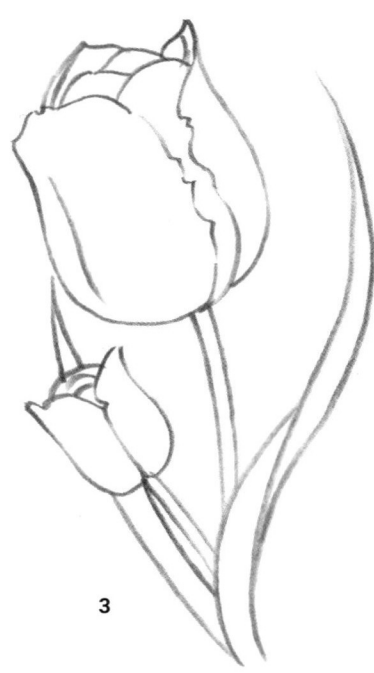

3

Apply shading to give this tulip depth,
or practice drawing more tulips below.

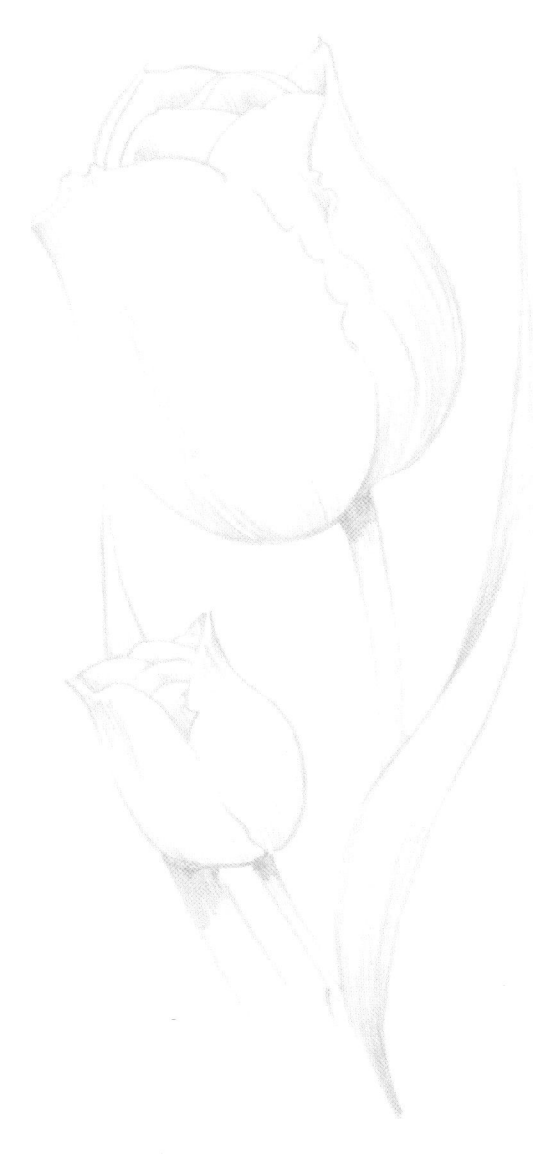

Bearded Iris

Of all the members of the iris family, the bearded iris is perhaps the most beautiful. Its flowers range in color from deep violet to blue and lavender to brilliant white. Some varieties are small, while others grow to about three feet tall.

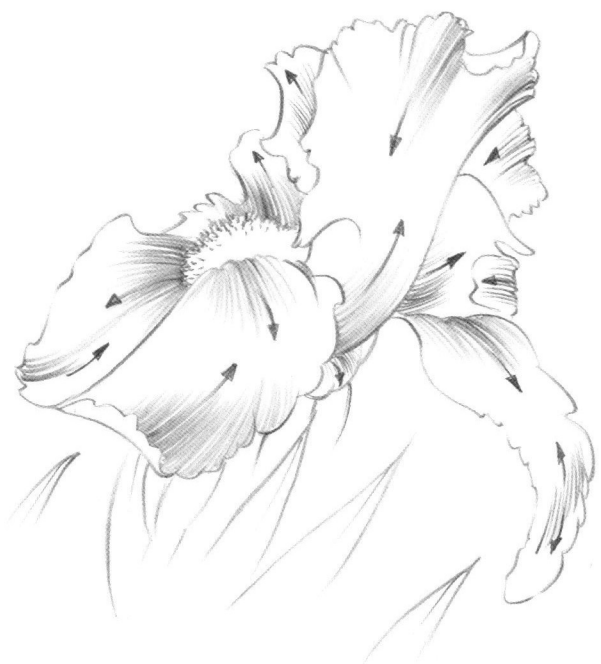

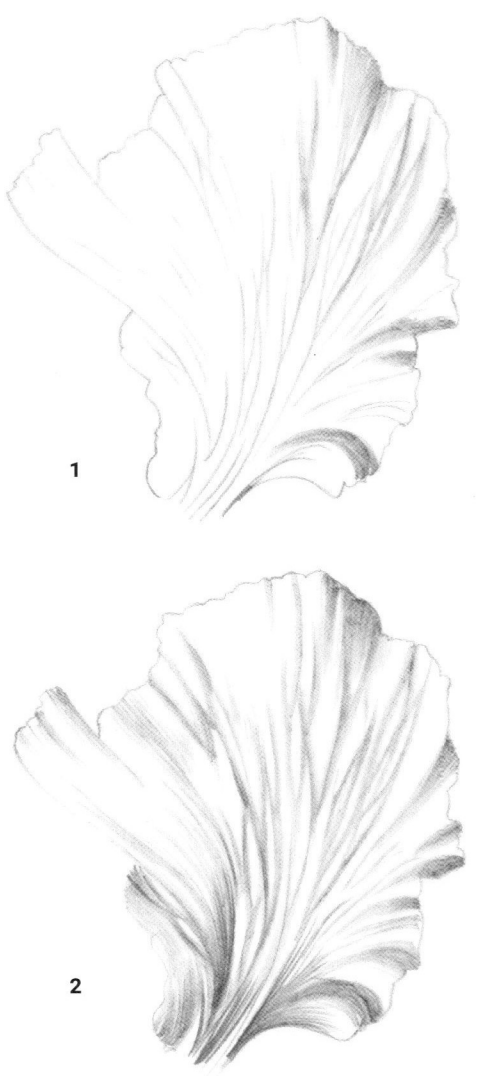

1

2

Follow the direction of the arrows when hatching the petals to make them appear lifelike. Use a sharp 2B pencil for the dark areas.

Drawing Petals To shade precisely, start with the curves of the petal, filling in its raised parts and then adding light shading over them. Use a blending stump to smooth and soften the shading.

Trace the drawing below, paying particular attention to the line work of the hatching, which is based on the shape of the leaves. Shade in the flower as desired, noting the darker areas of shadow.

Classic Rose

Many beginners are intimidated by drawing roses and other more complicated flowers, but there is nothing to fear. Simply start with basic shapes, as before, and build up the forms step by step.

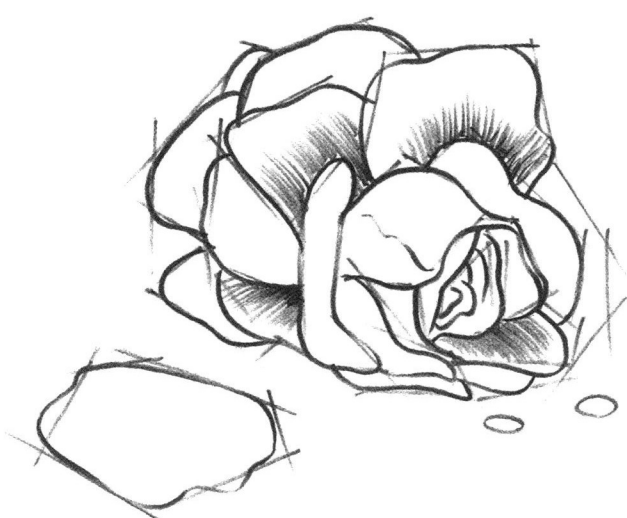

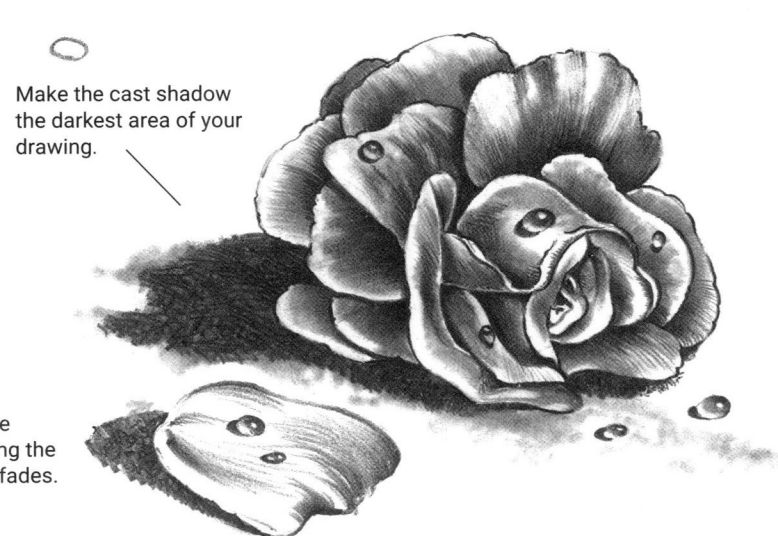

2 Begin shading by drawing strokes from inside each petal toward the outer edge.

Make the cast shadow the darkest area of your drawing.

1 Use an HB pencil to block in the overall shapes of the rose and petal, using a series of angular lines. Make all guidelines light so you won't have trouble removing or covering them later.

3 Now shade from the outer edge of each petal, meeting the strokes you drew in the opposite direction. Press firmly, lifting the pencil as the stroke comes to an end so that the line gently fades.

It takes practice to develop realistic shapes using shading.
Use the outlines below to practice shading the roses and petals.
Experiment with pressure to create various effects.

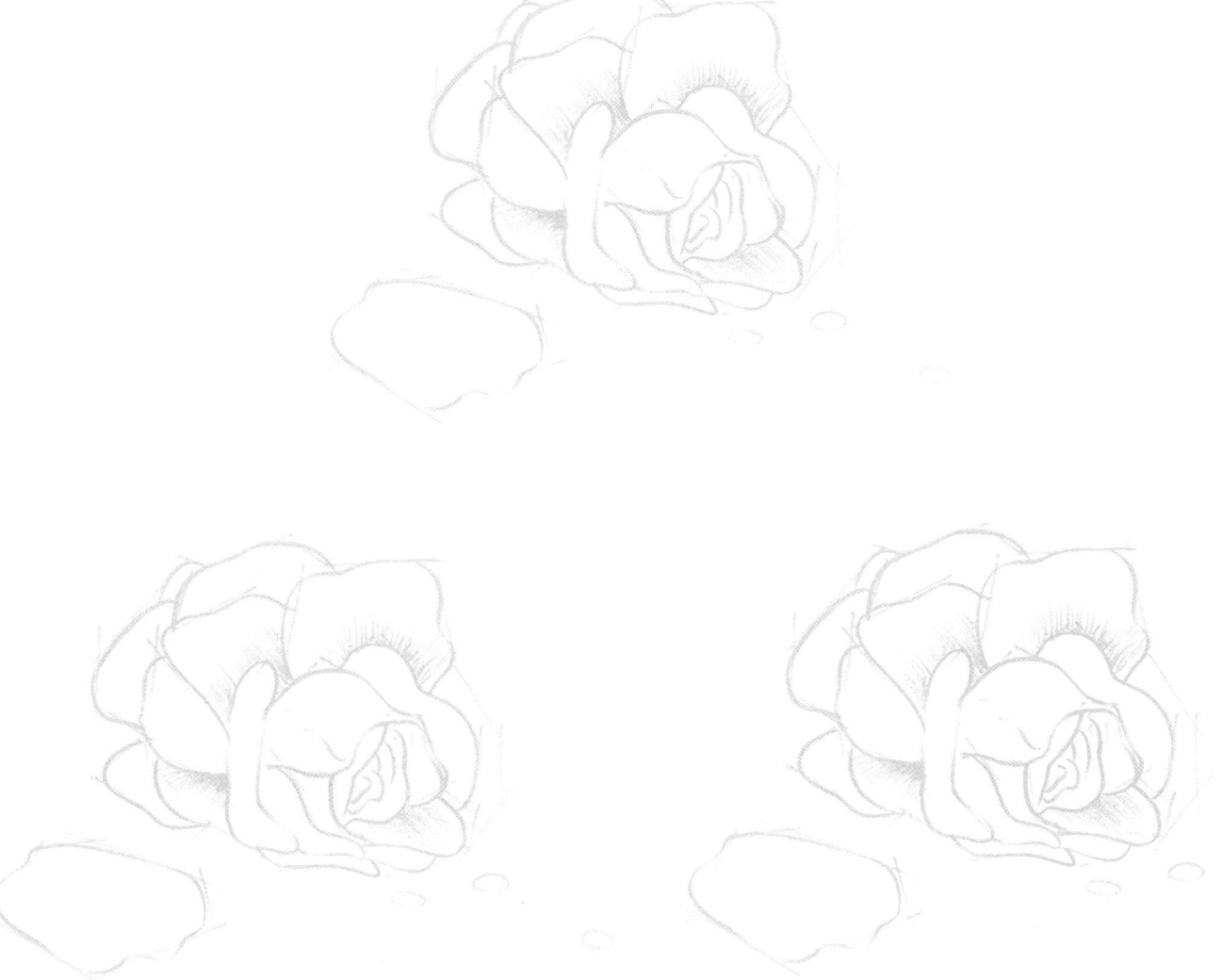

Primrose

Primroses delight us in spring with their vibrant colors. They are a wonderful example of a flower that bears multiple blossoms. Use the space below to draw a primrose. Take your time when drawing using basic lines to capture the shape of the flower.

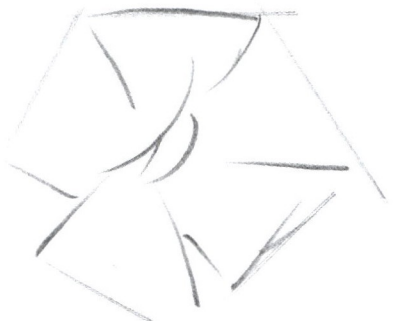 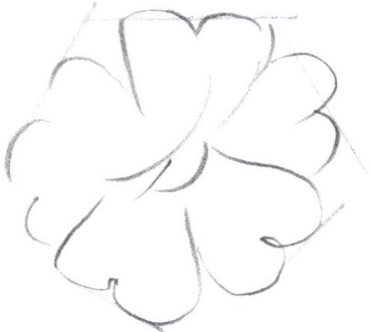 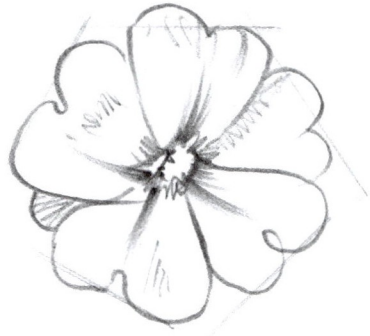

1 Take a close look at the primrose flower. Then, using light strokes and a sharp HB pencil, draw guidelines in the shape of a polygon.

2 Draw the outline of the flower with curved lines, adjusting the line thickness as needed.

3 Begin shading using a round pencil tip, following the shape of the flower. Apply darker shading toward the center of the flower.

Use the space below to continue drawing plants and flowers of your choice. Take a walk in nature and observe your surroundings. What types of flowers would you like to draw?

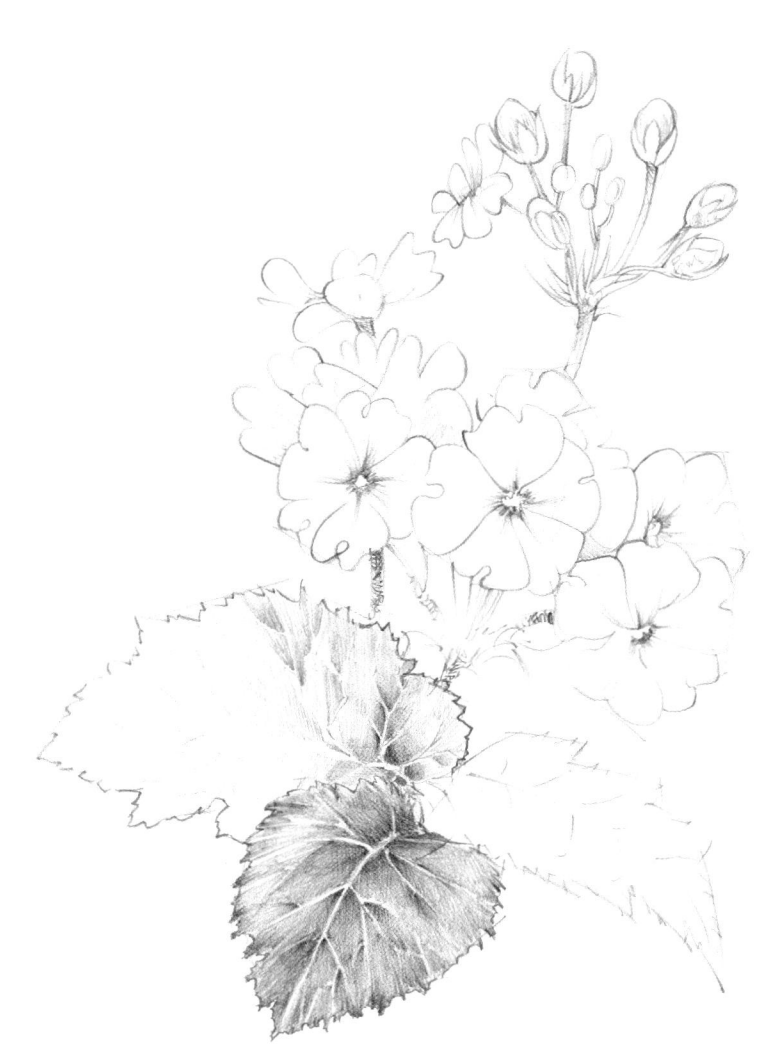

Basic Perspective

Creating depth or three-dimensional objects on a flat surface is based on the principle of perspective. The rules of perspective are guides for keeping objects in proper proportion to one another in a composition. The following exercise demonstrates the principles of one- and two-point perspective. Mastering perspective will add realism to your drawings. Let's review some basic terms.

Horizon Line (HL) The line that represents the viewer's eye level.

Vanishing Point (VP) The point on the horizon line where parallel lines, such as railroad tracks, appear to meet or converge.

One-Point Perspective You don't need horizontal lines to show one-point perspective; a vertical row of trees follows the same principle. Equally spaced objects, such as these trees and their cast shadows, appear to get closer together as they move toward the vanishing point.

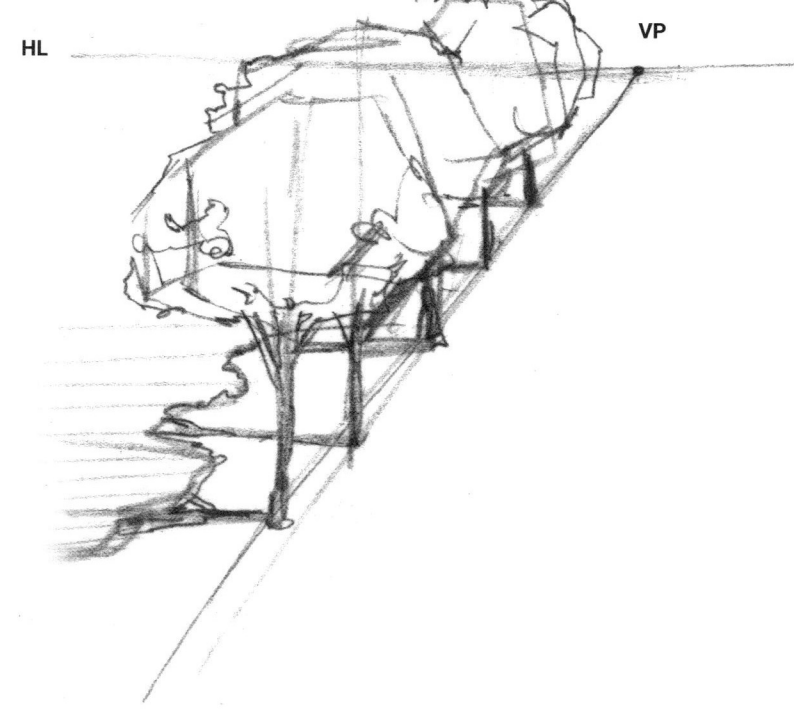

Using the perspective lines provided, draw a row of trees.

VP

HL

One- and Two-Point Perspective

One-Point Perspective

In one-point perspective, the face of a box is the closest part to the viewer, and it is parallel to the horizon line (eye level). The bottom, top, and sides of the face are parallel to the picture plane.

Two-Point Perspective

In two-point perspective, the corner of the box is close to the viewer. Therefore, two vanishing points on the horizon are needed. In this perspective, nothing is parallel to the horizon.

Horizon line

1 Draw a horizontal line, and label it "eye level" or "horizon line." Draw a box below this line.

VP

2 Now draw a light guideline from the top-right corner to a spot on the horizon line. Place a dot there, and label it VP (vanishing point). All side lines will go to the same VP.

VP

3 Next, draw a line from the other corner as shown, and then draw a horizontal line to establish the back of the box.

VP

4 Finally, darken all lines as shown, and you will have drawn a perfect box in one-point perspective. This box may become a book, a chest, a building, etc.

VP   **Horizon line**   **VP**

1 Establish the horizon line, and then place a dot at each end. Draw a vertical line that represents the corner of the box closest to the viewer.

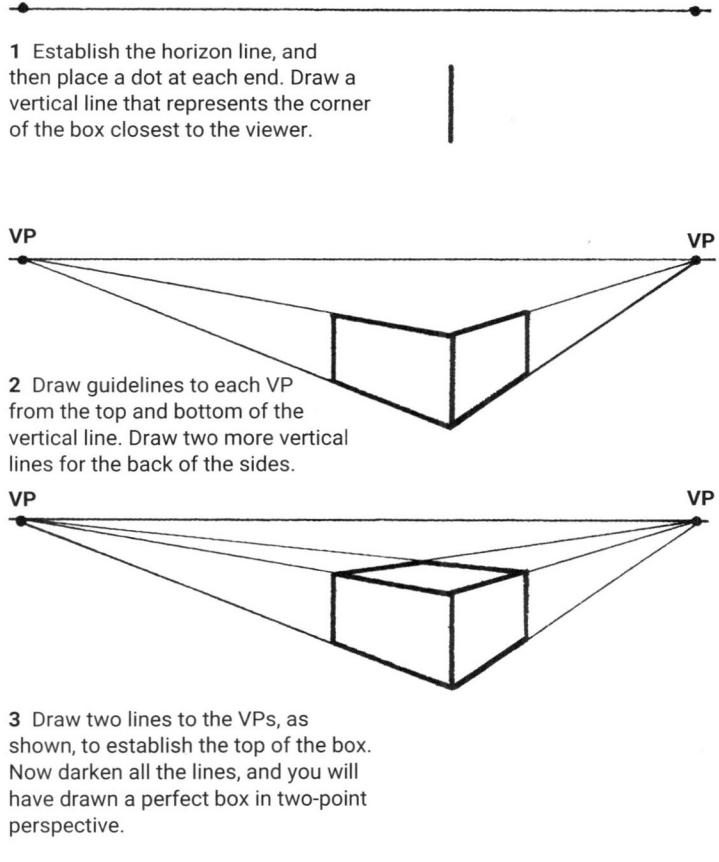

VP   **VP**

2 Draw guidelines to each VP from the top and bottom of the vertical line. Draw two more vertical lines for the back of the sides.

VP   **VP**

3 Draw two lines to the VPs, as shown, to establish the top of the box. Now darken all the lines, and you will have drawn a perfect box in two-point perspective.

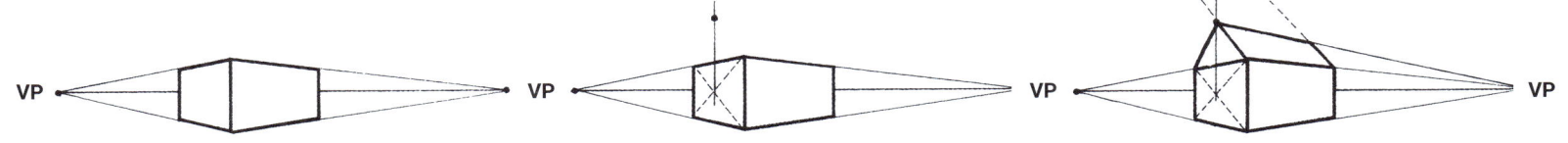

1 Draw a box in two-point perspective.

2 Find the center of the face by drawing diagonal lines from corner to corner; then draw a vertical line upward through the center. Make a dot for the roof height.

3 Using the vanishing point, draw a line for the angle of the roof ridge; then draw the back of the roof. The angled roof lines will meet at a third VP somewhere in the sky.

Use the space below to draw a building in two-point perspective.

Landscapes in Perspective

To create a realistic landscape, you should be familiar with some basic principles of perspective. In the line drawing below, the horizontal edges of the planes move closer together as they recede to the left and right, eventually merging at vanishing points outside the picture area. Sketch some simple boxes for practice, moving on to more involved subjects, such as buildings.

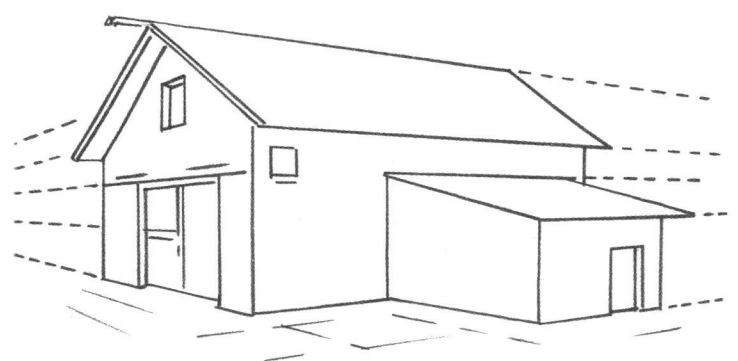

1 Draw the barn following the rules of perspective.

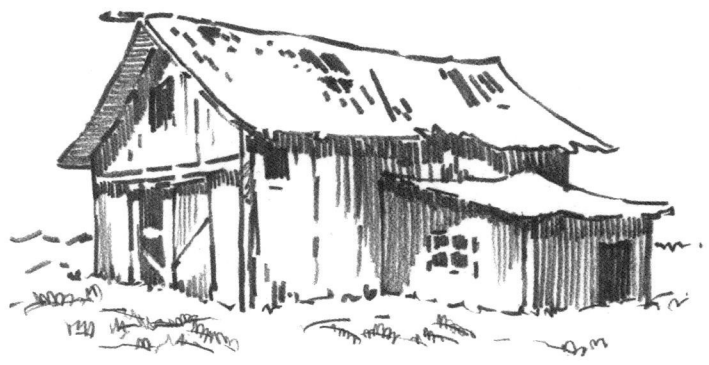

2 Once the basic shapes are in place, add details and shading.

Use the outline below to practice drawing a structure in perspective.

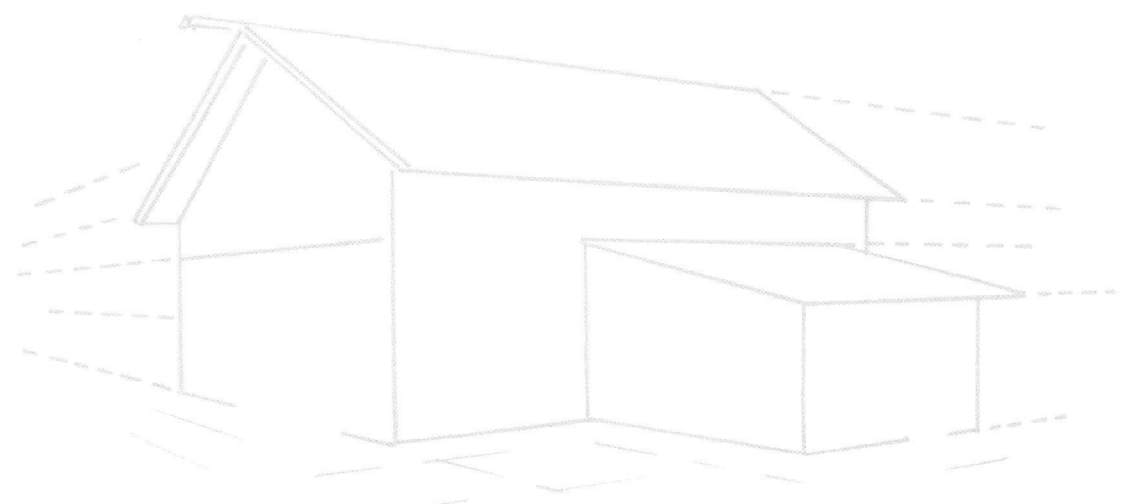

Drawing Trees

When drawing trees, whether from references or from nature, work out the basic shapes with simple line drawings. Broad-leaved trees—such as beeches, maples, and some oaks—have flat leaves and produce flowers, as well as shed their leaves every fall. Study the subtle variations of shapes shown in the examples below. As you draw, notice the different techniques used for the leaves on each tree. First sketch the trunk, and then draw the general shape of the whole group of leaves before shading the foliage.

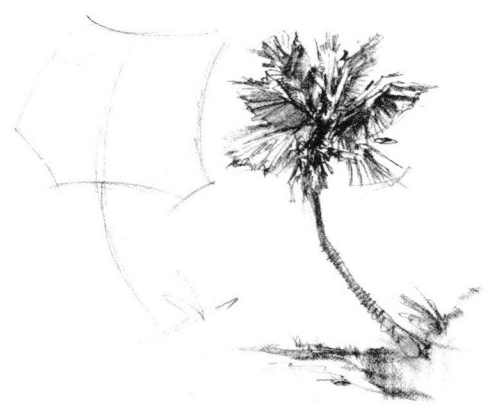
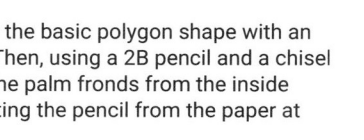
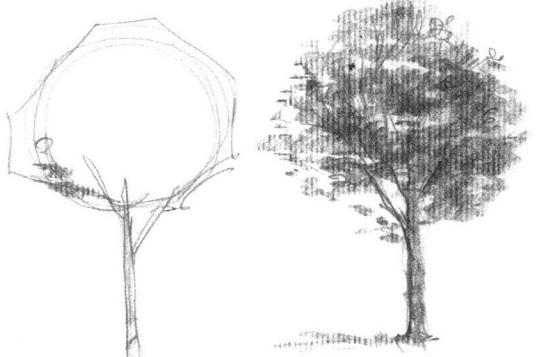
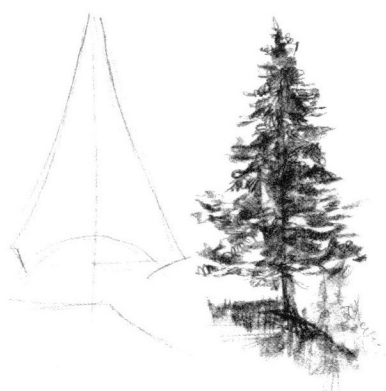

Palm Draw the basic polygon shape with an HB pencil. Then, using a 2B pencil and a chisel tip, create the palm fronds from the inside outward, lifting the pencil from the paper at the end.

Maple Use an HB pencil to draw the circle for the crown. Then, using the side of the lead, shade the leaves, applying varying pressure. Finally, add details with a sharp pencil.

Spruce Draw the basic triangular shape with an HB pencil. Then, using a 2B pencil with a round tip, add the branches with short horizontal strokes. Draw details with a sharp HB pencil.

Take a walk in your neighborhood and observe the trees,
including the shapes of their trunks, branches, and leaves.
Draw your observations below.

Basic Tree Shape

Sketch the basic shapes of this tree using the tip of an HB pencil. Use a
2B pencil to shade the dark areas behind the branches to create depth.
Continue adding darker values, and begin to suggest the leaves. Notice
how the variations of values create depth in the final drawing.

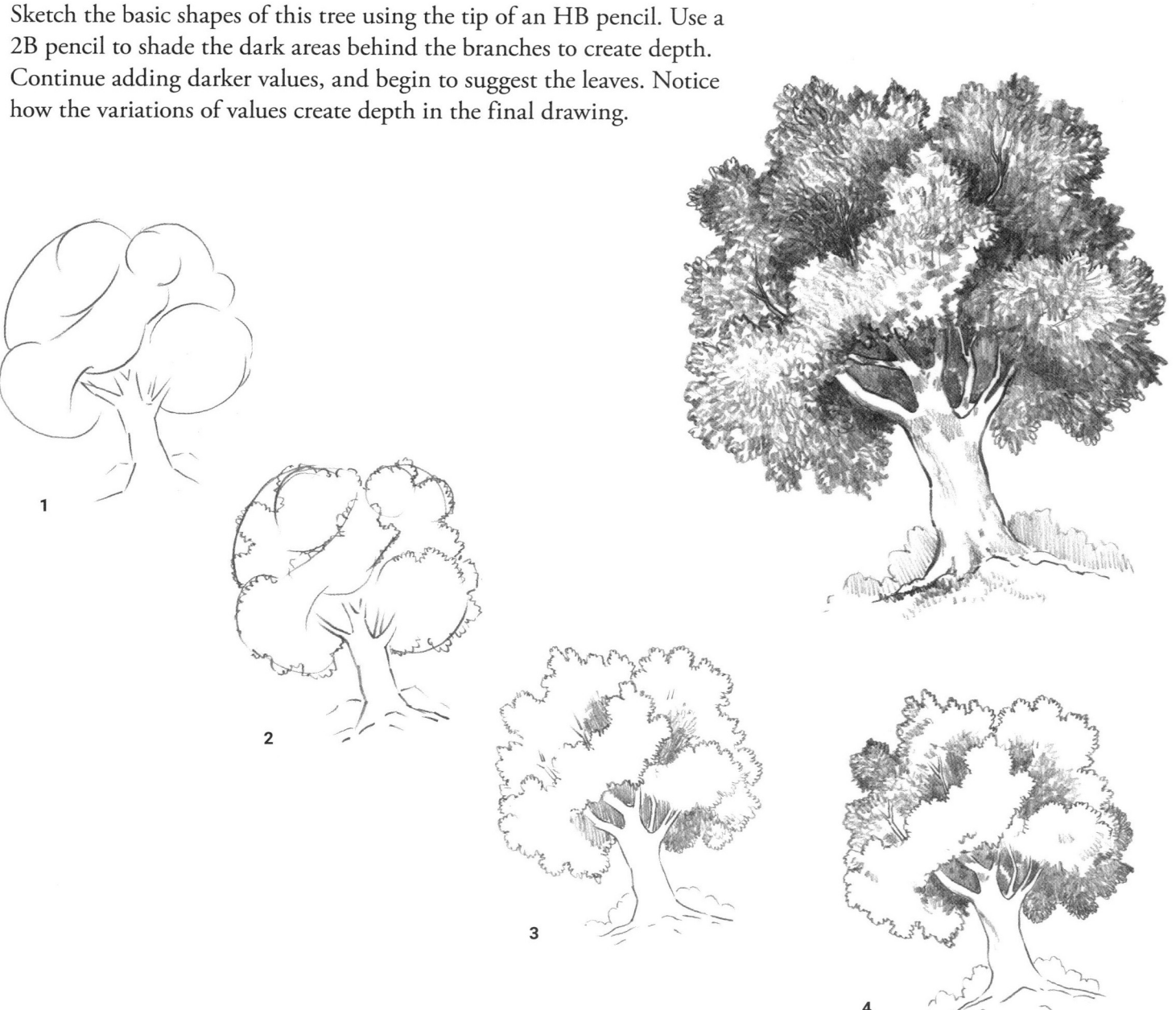

Use the outline below to practice drawing a basic tree.

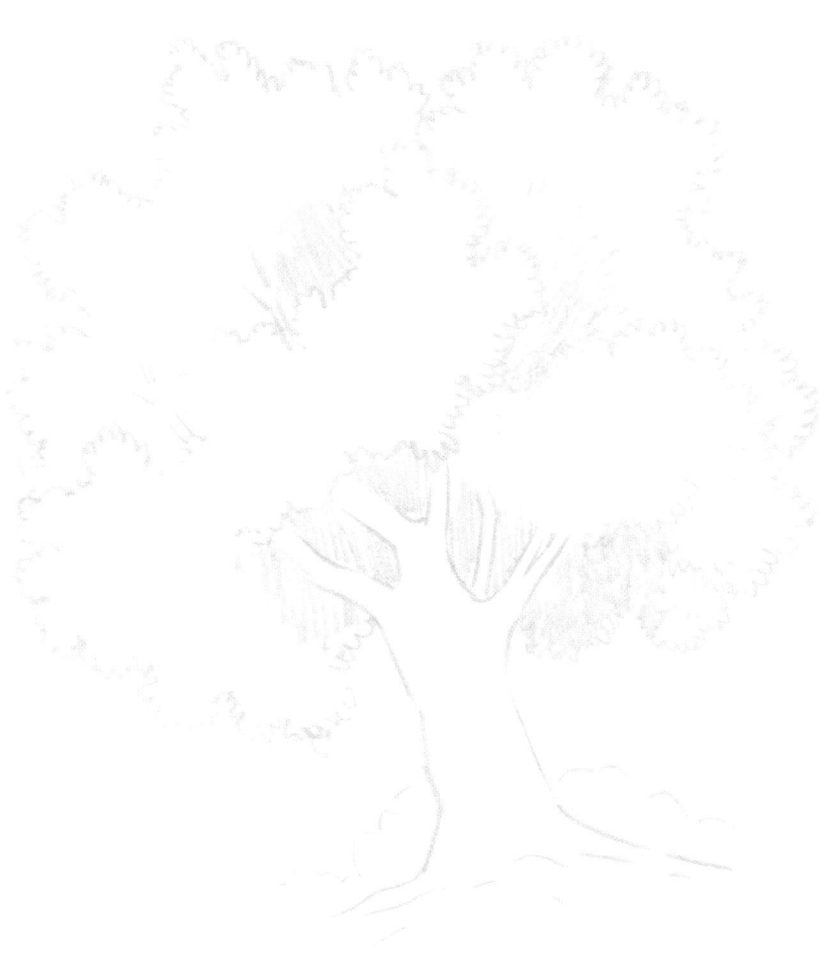

Branches and Twigs

As trees grow, they become taller and thicker, but each tree grows in its own distinctive way. In trees with large leaves, the trunk branches out into many gnarled branches. Conifers like spruce trees tend to grow at regular intervals. Draw a rough sketch of the branch, noting changes in the direction of growth. Build up the forms of the tree and finish with shading. Use broken and irregular strokes to make the branches appear natural.

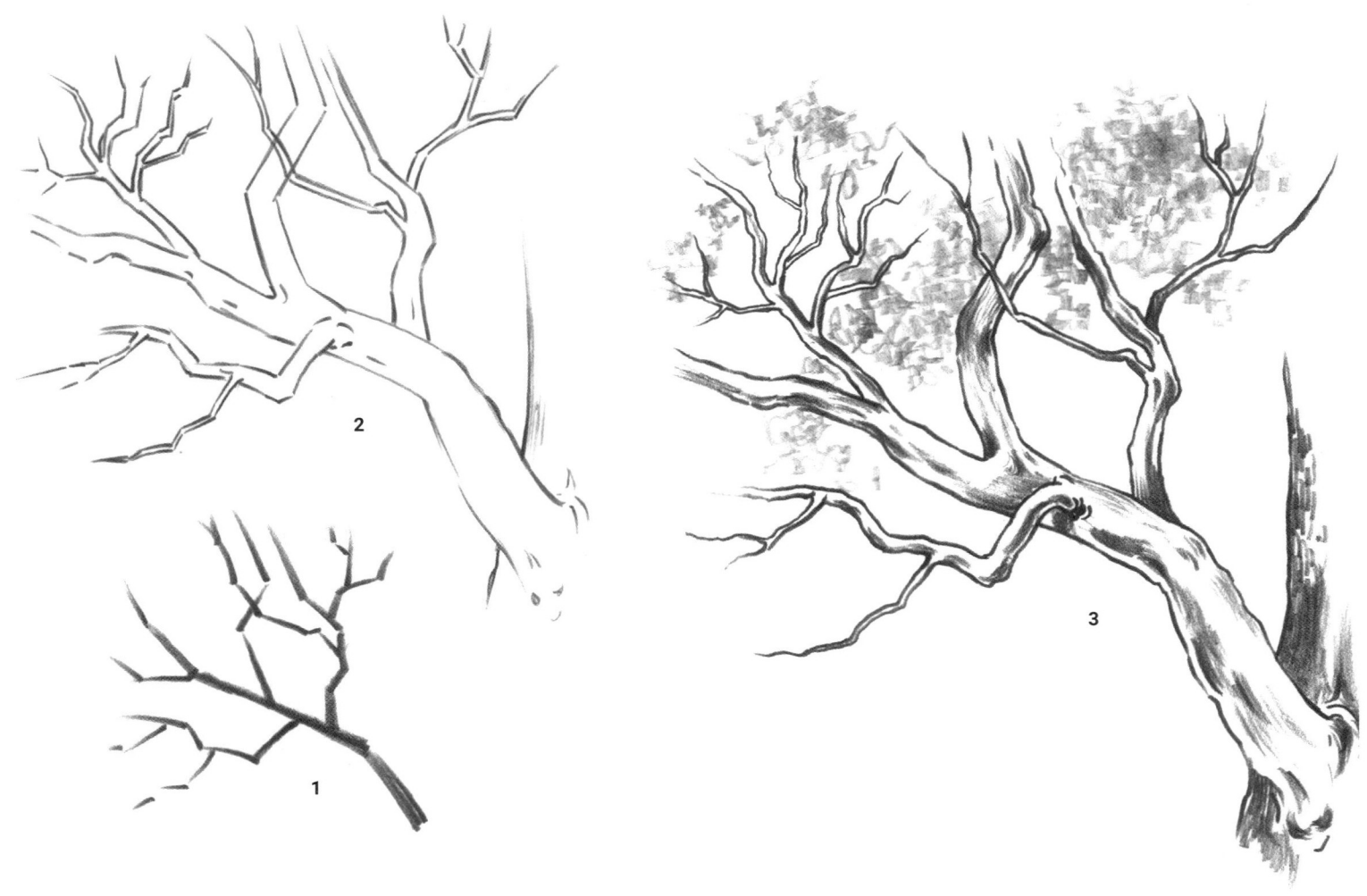

Examine this tree trunk and branches. Continue to add to the drawing with twigs and foliage. Don't forget to add elements to the foreground and background, such as fallen leaves and broken twigs.

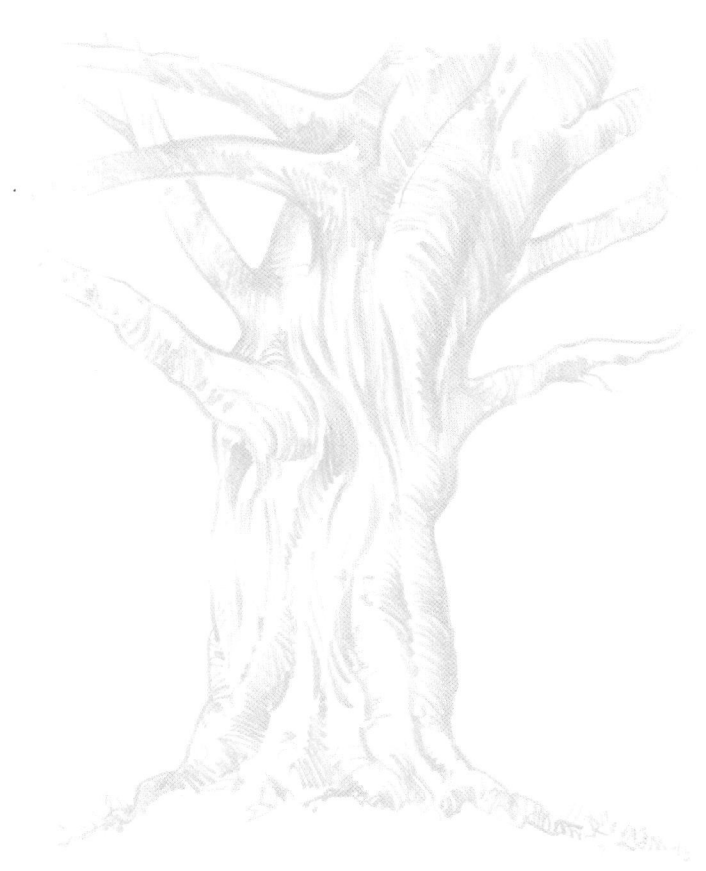

Roots

Roots grow down and outward to anchor the tree in the ground. These root patterns have twists and bumps, which make them interesting to draw. Study the root pattern shown. Lightly sketch the outlines and basic shapes with an HB pencil. Shape the roots with small curved lines. Using the side of a 2B pencil, darken some of the curved lines to give the roots a more natural appearance.

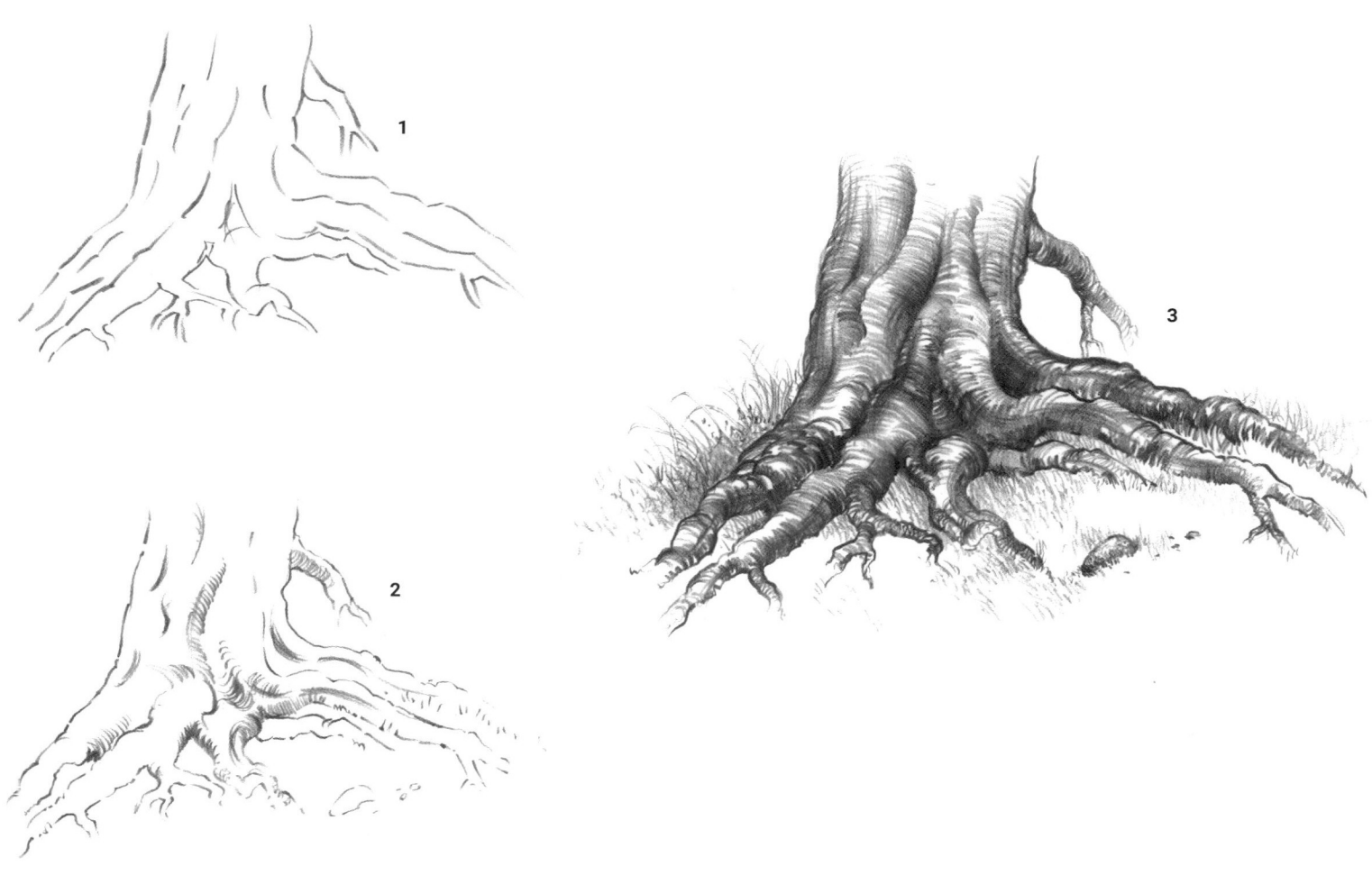

Use the outline below to practice drawing root patterns.
Add shading to make the drawing more lifelike.

Fallen Tree

Apply your previously acquired knowledge to draw this giant fallen tree. Note where shading and hatching creates depth and dimension.

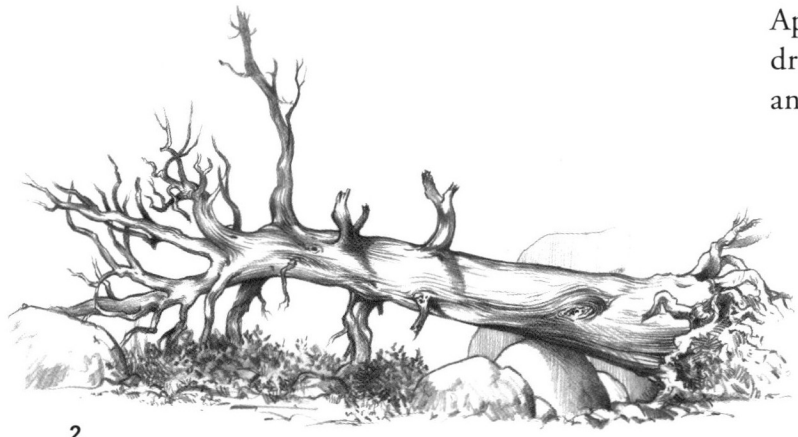

2

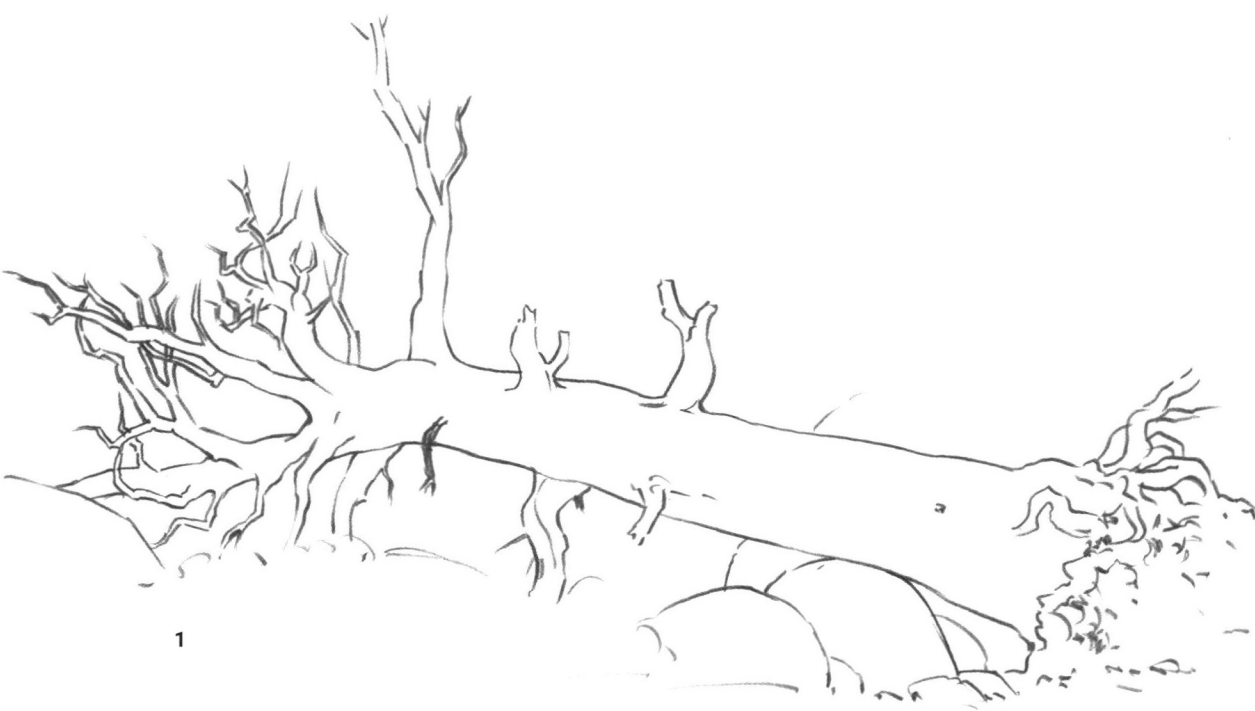

1

Take a hike in nature and look for a fallen tree.
Draw your observations here.

Textured Surfaces

To render textured surfaces, such as rocks, start by lightly blocking in the basic shapes to establish the different planes. Use a variety of oddly shaped and uneven lines so your rocks don't appear flat and unnatural.

Creating Texture Rock surfaces are generally uneven and bumpy. Try to create a variety of shading values on the rocks so they appear jagged. Hatch in various directions to follow the shapes of the rocks, and make the values darker in the deepest crevices, on sharp edges, and in the areas between the rocks.

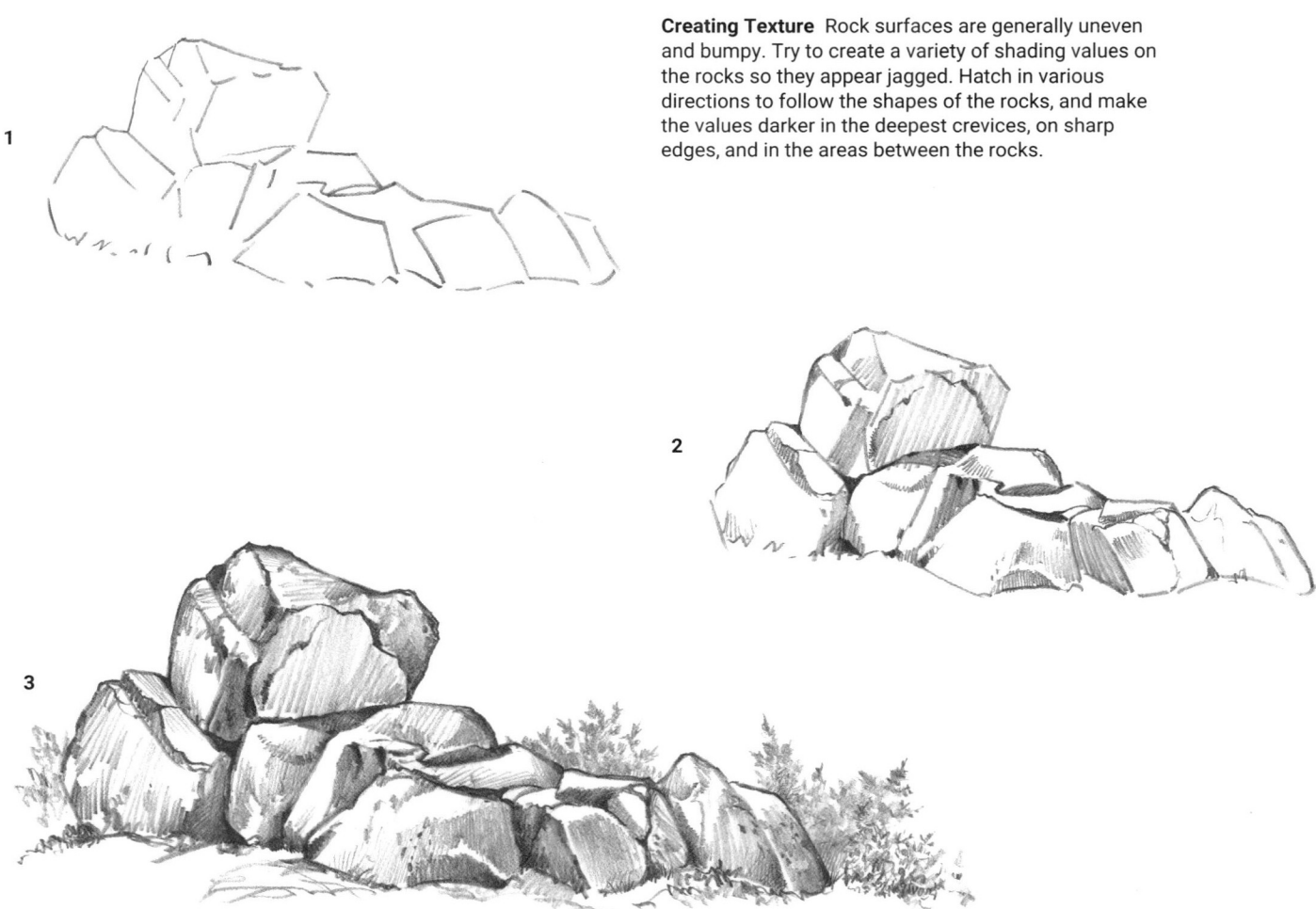

Use hatching to create rough, uneven surfaces.
Add dense shading where the shadows are deepest,
such as in gaps, on edges, and in notches.

Clouds

Clouds are great elements to include in a landscape because they can set the mood of the drawing. Some clouds create a dramatic mood, while others evoke a calm feeling.

Sketching Cloud Formations Using light pressure and a 2B pencil, sketch the outline of the clouds. Then, using the broad side of the pencil, shade the area of the sky around the cloud. This will make the clouds appear full and soft.

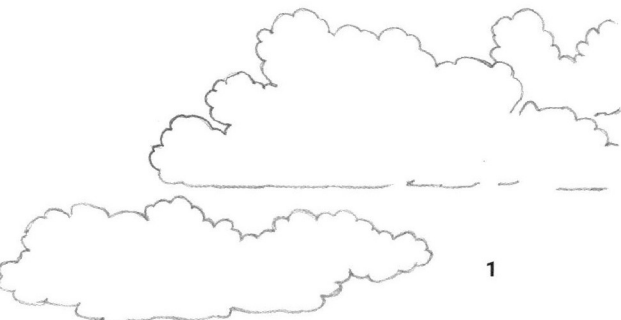

1

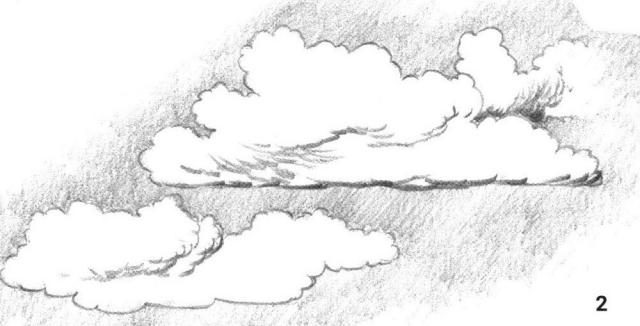

2

Study a variety of cloud shapes and practice drawing them. Try to create soft, light-looking clouds and wisps as well as long, thin, gray clouds. Look for unusual clouds in the sky and draw them.

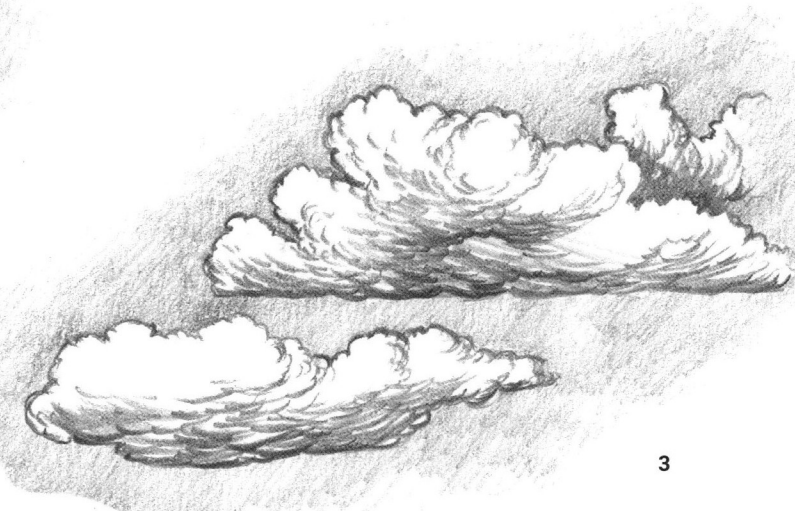

3

Use the outline below to practice drawing cloud formations.
Observe clouds in the sky, and try to capture them
in your sketchbook.

Landscape Composition

Most landscapes have a background, middle ground, and foreground. The background represents areas that are farthest in distance; it leads to the foreground, the areas that appear closest in distance. The background, middle ground, and foreground do not have to take up equal space in a composition. Below, the middle ground and foreground are placed low, so the elements in the background become the area of interest. Overlapping subjects, such as trees and rocks, help create a feeling of depth.

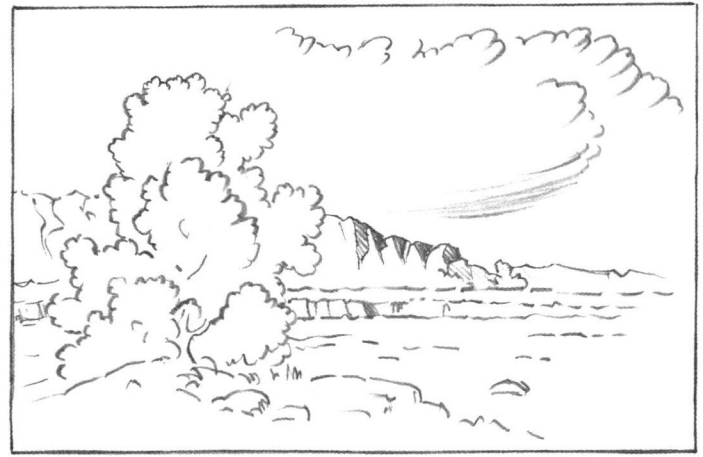

1 Sketch a simple landscape composition, lightly blocking out a background, middle ground, and foreground.

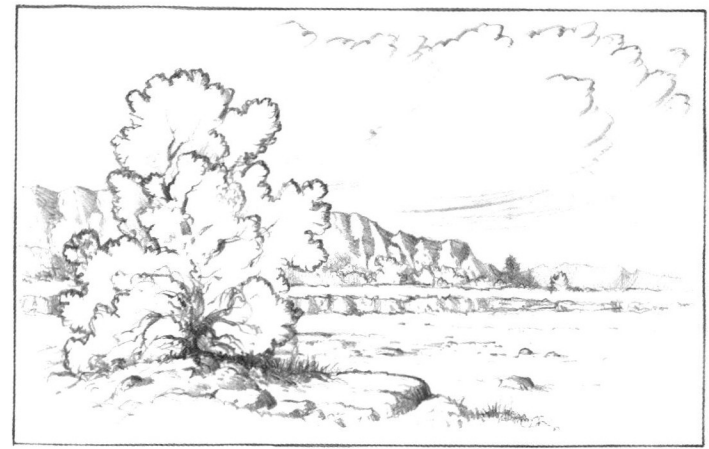

2 Begin to lightly fill in the shapes, but avoid getting overly detailed. The eye should be able to enjoy the whole without jumping from detail to detail.

Use this outline to create a simple landscape composition.

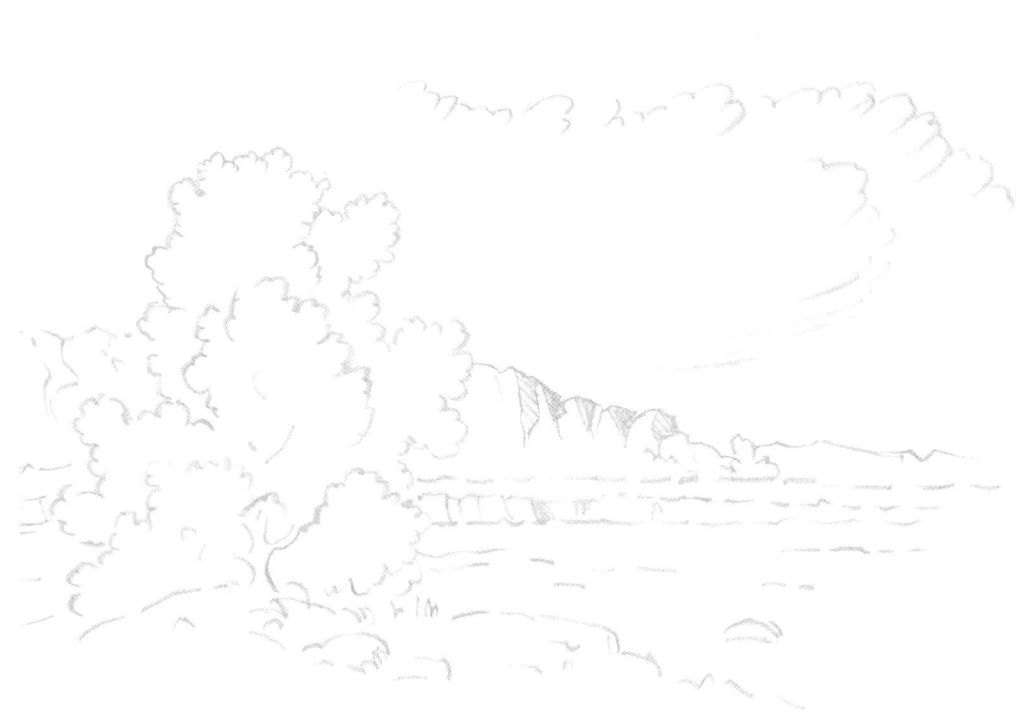

Depth and Distance

The illusion of depth is obvious in this line drawing; the road narrows as it travels back into the distance, and the hills overlap each other. To offset the slanting curves of the hills and foliage, a structure was placed just to the right of center. Practice creating the illusion of depth by sketching some overlapping elements similar to the ones in this landscape. Vary the lines for the areas representing foliage and trees, and make them appear bumpy and bushy. For the road, draw two relatively straight lines that move closer together as they recede.

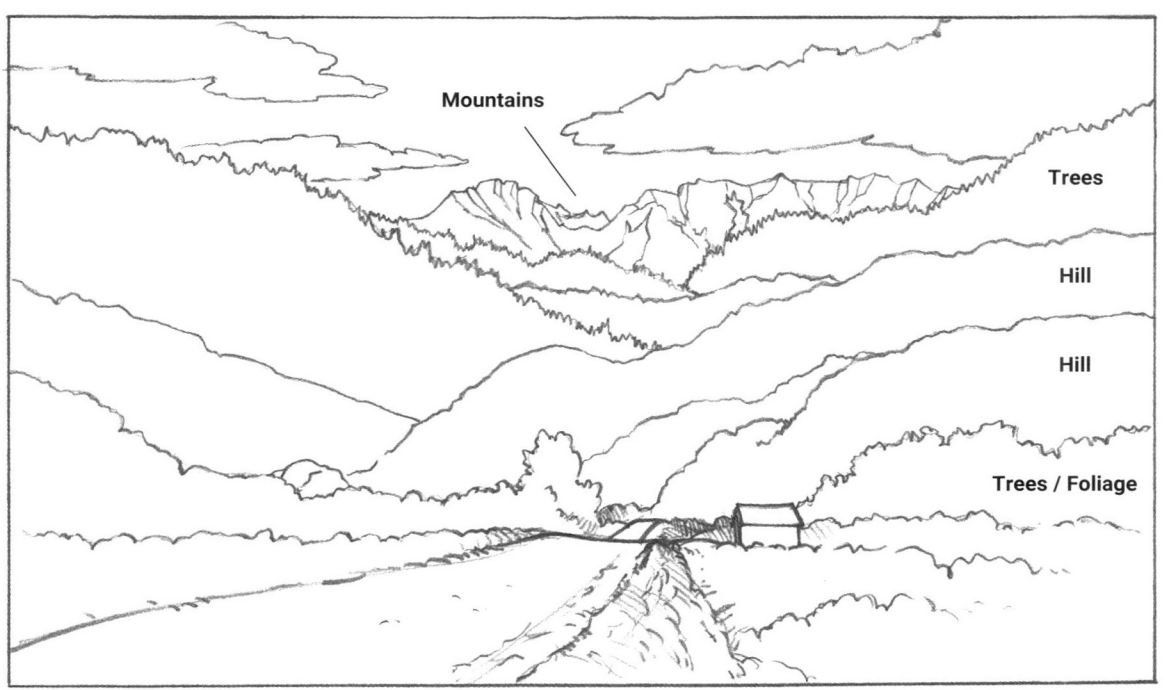

Continue to add details to the landscape below, adding texture, shading, and highlights to bring it to life. Add animals and people to the scene, if you like, making sure they stay in proper perspective.

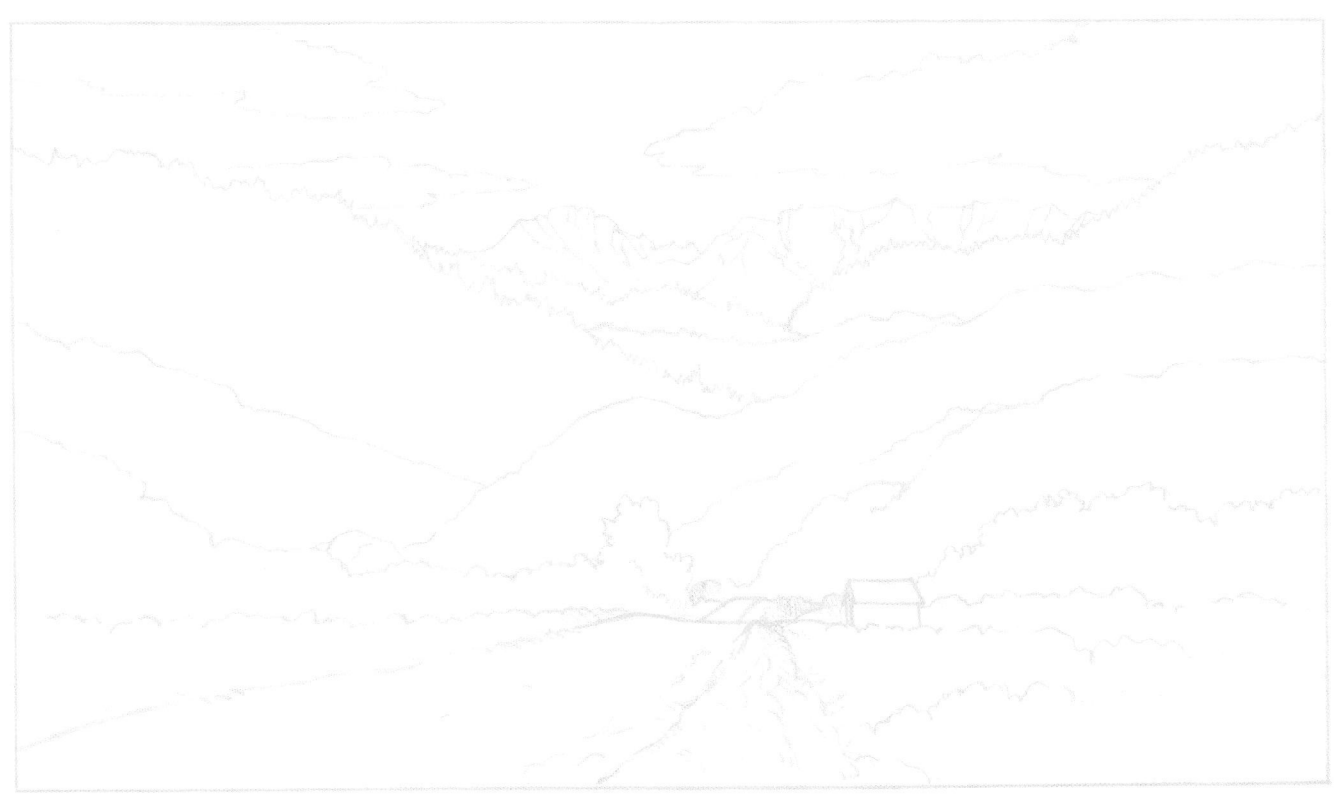

Creek with Rocks

Drawing landscapes containing creeks and rocks is a great way to improve artistic skills because of the variety of surface textures. It's imperative that your preliminary drawing accurately shows depth through proper perspective and incorporating a pleasing balance of overlapping elements.

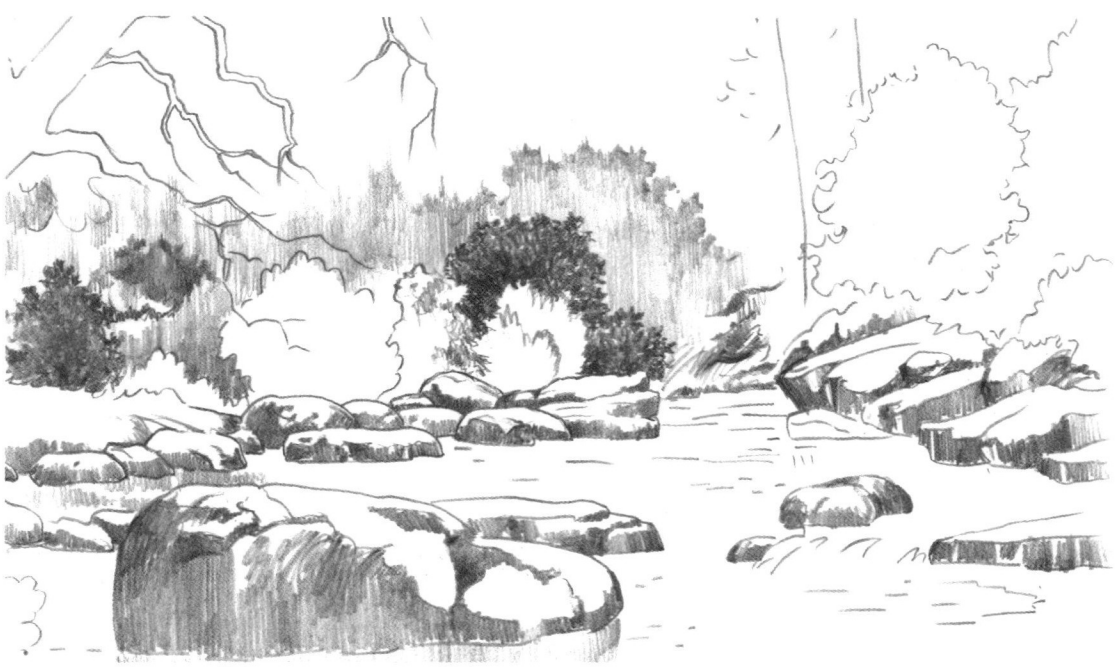

Basic Sketch Begin shading the trees in the distance; then work your way to the middle ground and foreground. Don't completely shade each object before moving to the next one. Work on the entire drawing so it maintains a sense of unity. You don't want one area to appear as though you spent more time on it. Even though there are many light and dark areas throughout the drawing, the degree of shading should remain relatively consistent.

Use this outline to build out the creek landscape.

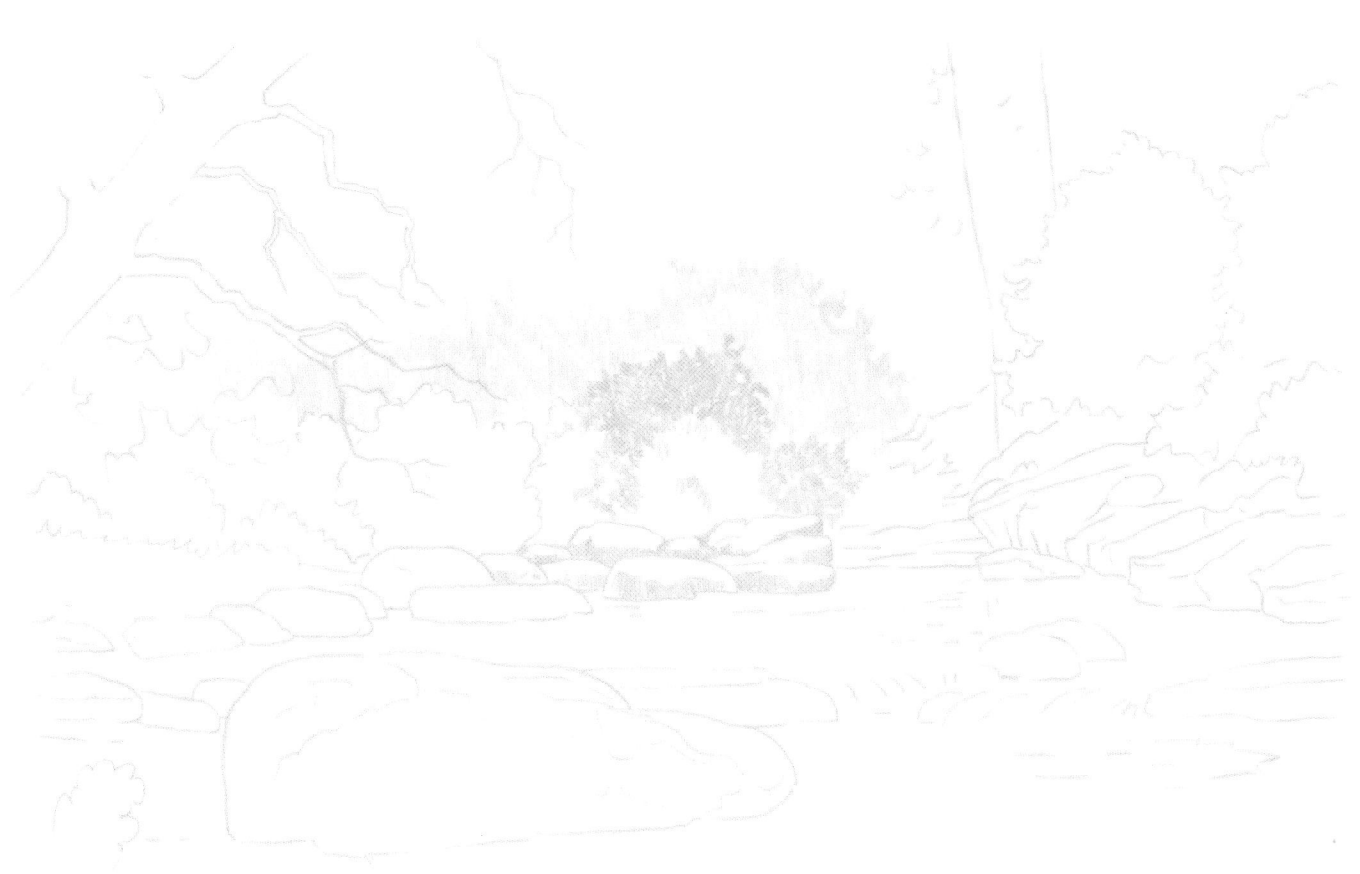

Adding Foliage

Foliage is an ideal background for stones, as the vibrant nature of leaves and shrubs contrasts beautifully against smooth and textured rock. Draw the outlines of the surrounding foliage, and then add subtle detail using some of the techniques you've learned so far.

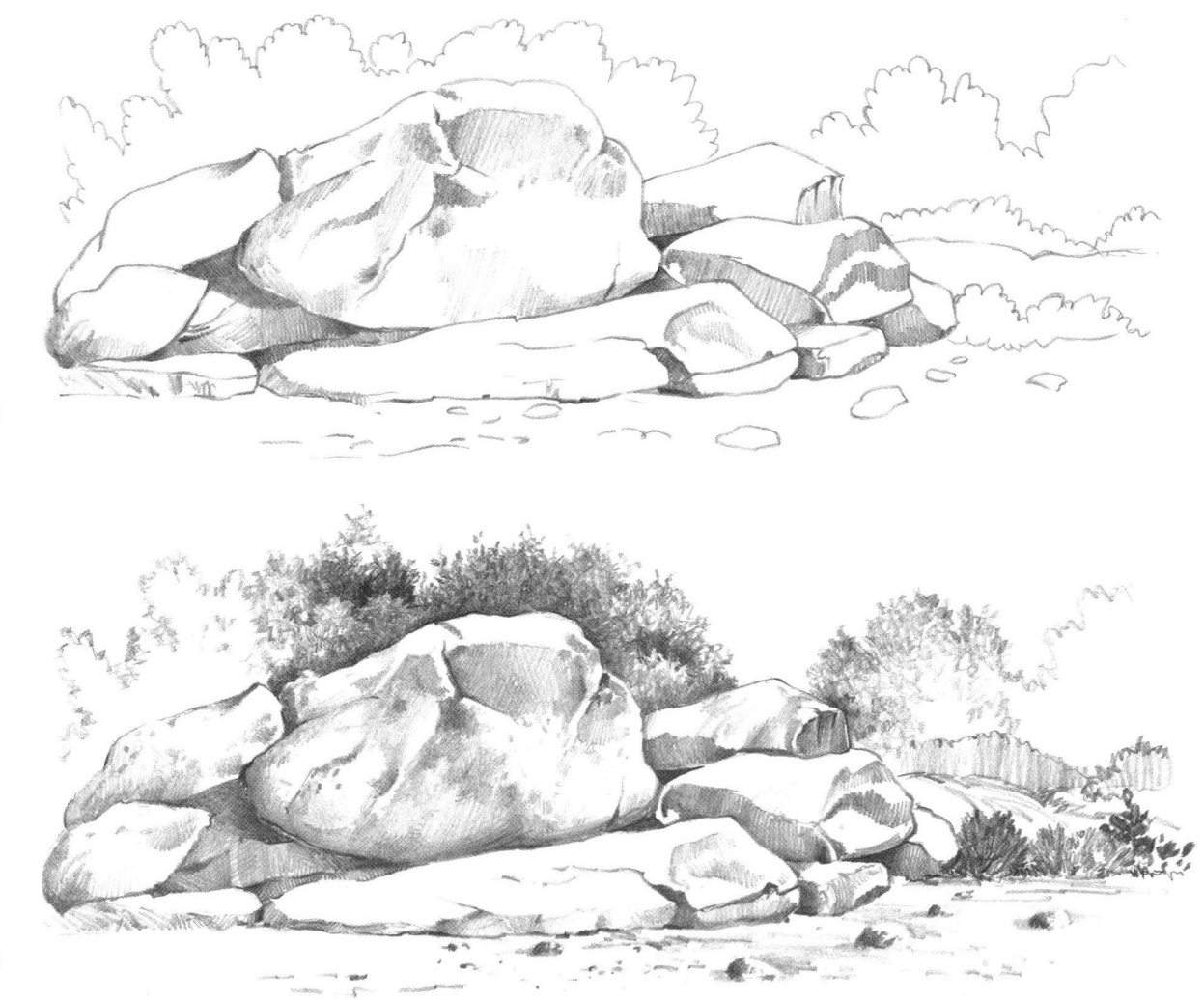

1

2

Shade the boulders, and detail the foliage, trees, and shrubs. Use the finished drawing as a guide, or build on the template and create your own scene.

Mountains

A mountain landscape can be blocked in with a few simple lines as shown in step one. Refine the shapes into the rugged mountains shown in step two, keeping in mind that it isn't necessary to include every curvature you see. Remember that deep mountain crevices should be shaded in darker tones to bring out their rocky texture.

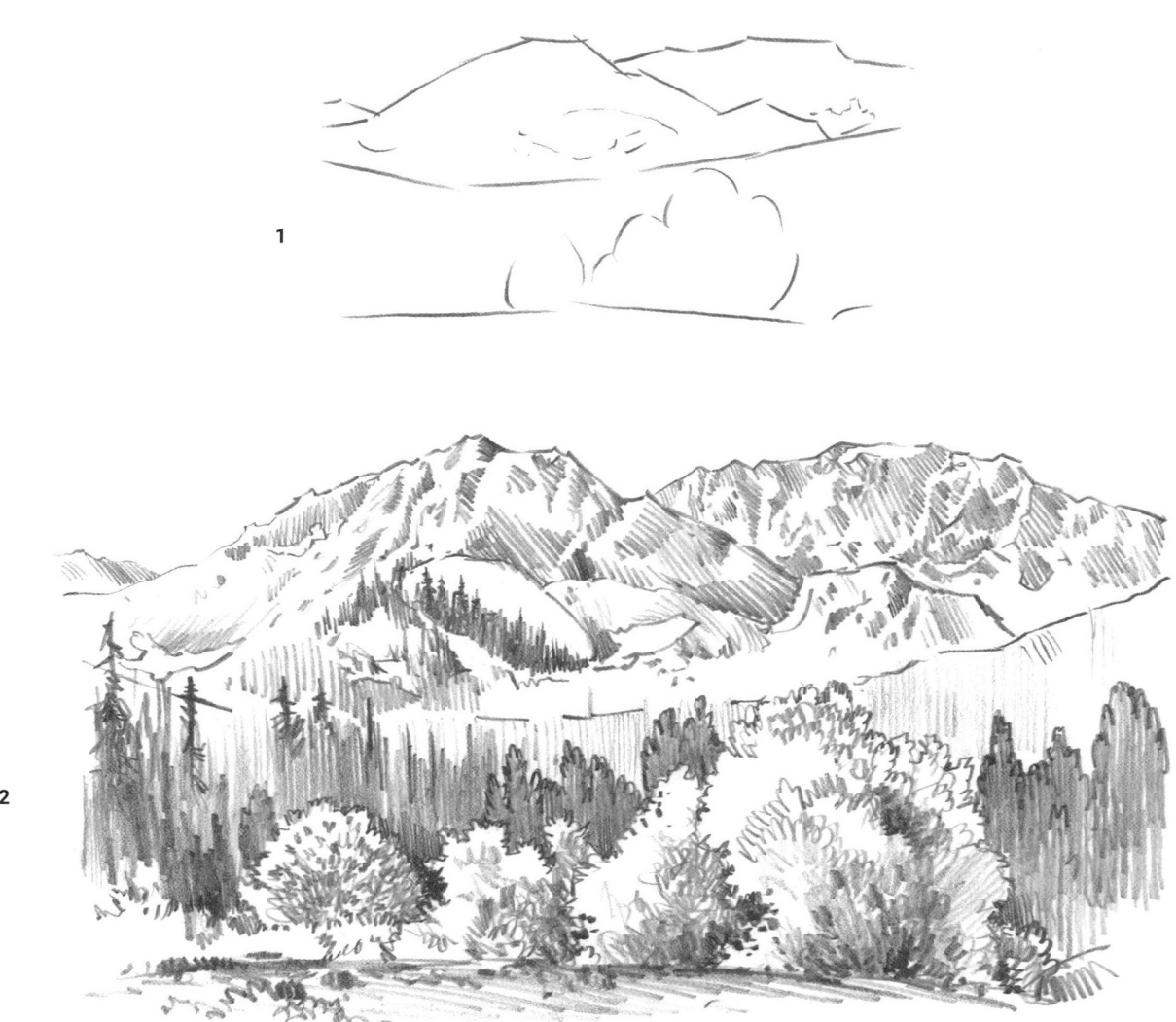

Use shading and hatching to complete the mountain drawing.

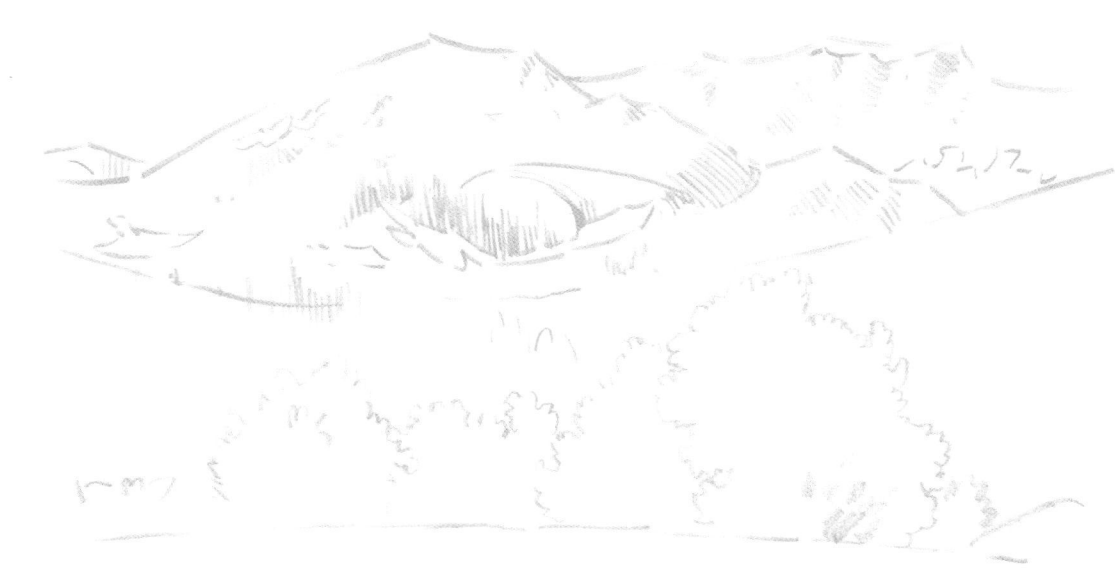

Forest Path

The small cottage at the side of the forest path is the focal point of this idyllic scene. The trees and vegetation seem to envelop the dwelling, which consists of straight, linear shapes. The contrast makes for an interesting scene.

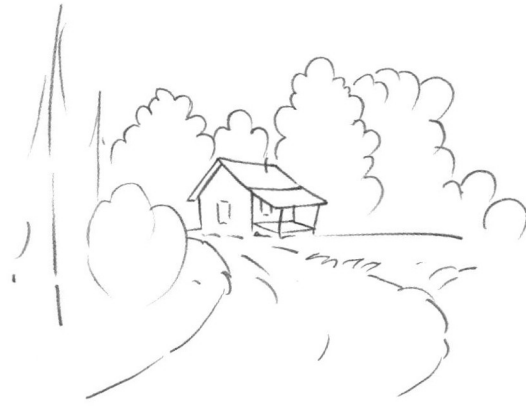

1 Sketch the scene using basic lines and shapes.

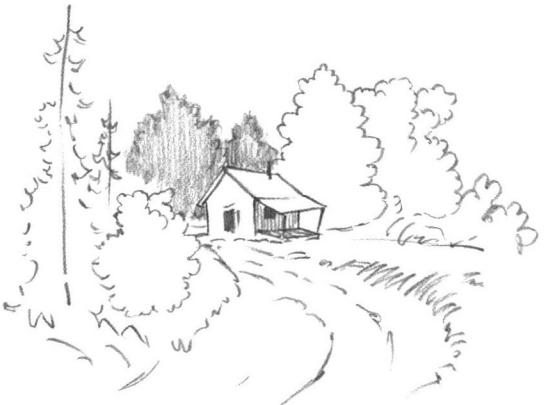

2 Begin to develop the details with light shading.

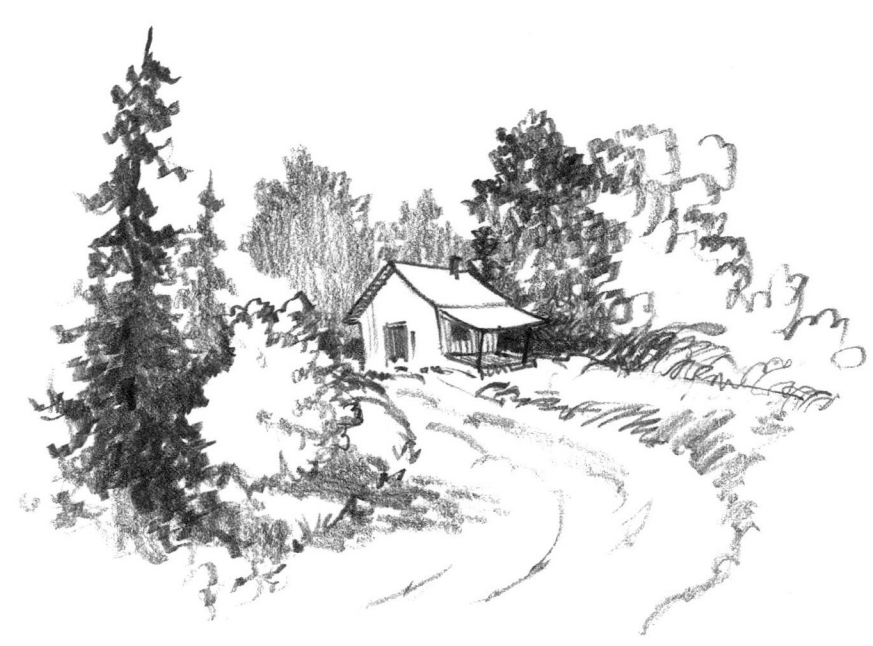

3 Work your way around the drawing, developing the trees, cottage, and surrounding landscape.

Now it's your turn! Practice building out this landscape from preliminary sketch to finished drawing.

Negative Space

Sometimes it's easier to draw the area around an object instead of drawing the object itself. The area around and between objects is called "negative space." (The actual objects are called "positive space.") When you draw the negative shapes around an object, you're also creating the edges of the object at the same time. The examples below are simple demonstrations of how to draw negative space. Try sketching the negative space, and notice how the objects seem to emerge almost magically from the shadows!

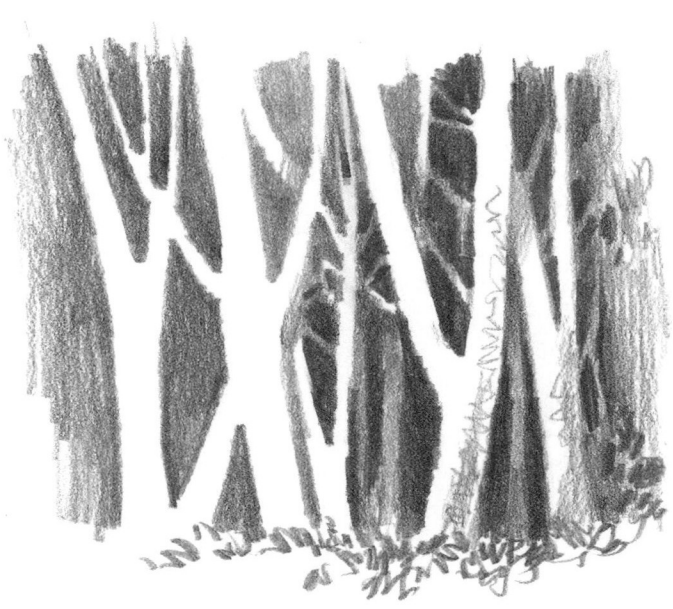

Filling In To draw this fence, first fill the space between the pickets with the wide side of the pencil lead. Once the fence has taken shape, add some hatching to the upper rail on the right. This will further intensify the play of light and shadow.

Silhouetting This small group of trees is a little more difficult to draw than the fence on the left. But once you've sketched the trunks, the task becomes easier. The shadows between the trunks are of varying density, adding interest to the image.

Negative space is an exciting way to draw objects.
Use the space below to practice this technique.

Animal Textures

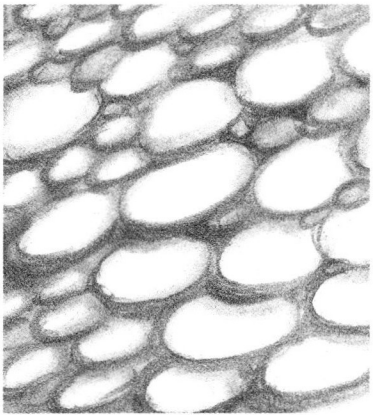

Smooth Scales To depict smooth scales, first draw ovals of various sizes; then shade between them. Because scales overlap, be sure to partially cover each scale with the next layer.

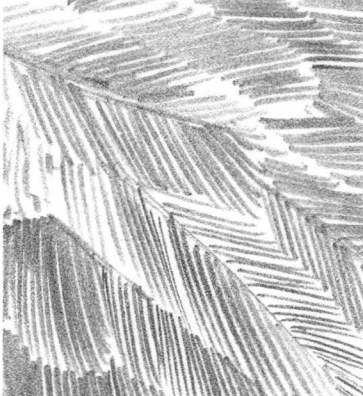

Fine Feathers For light, downy feathers, apply thin, parallel lines along the feather stems to form a series of V shapes. Avoid crisp outlines, which can take away from the softness.

Fur Draw short, shimmering fur with small strokes and the broad side of your pencil. Create small wrinkles by adding a few horizontal bands that are lighter than the rest of the fur.

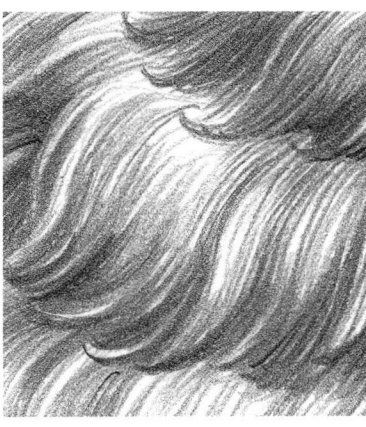

Wavy Hair For layers of soft curls, stroke in S-shaped lines that end in tighter curves. Leave the highlights free of graphite, and stroke with more pressure as you move to the shadows.

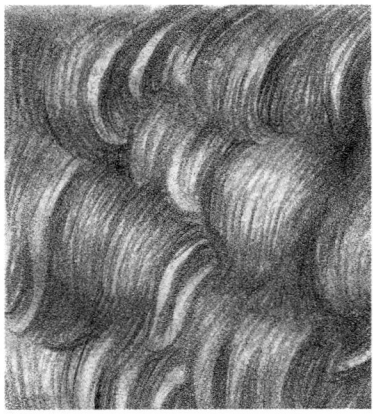

Curly Hair Curly, woolly coats can be drawn with overlapping circular strokes of varying values. For realism, draw curls of differing shapes and sizes, and blend for softness.

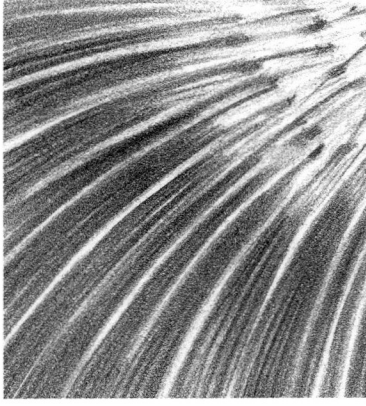

Whiskers First, draw small dots around the muzzle. Then shape the fur. Use a kneaded eraser and neatly lift out long, curved lines.

Draw animal fur, hair, and feathers in the boxes below.

Feathers

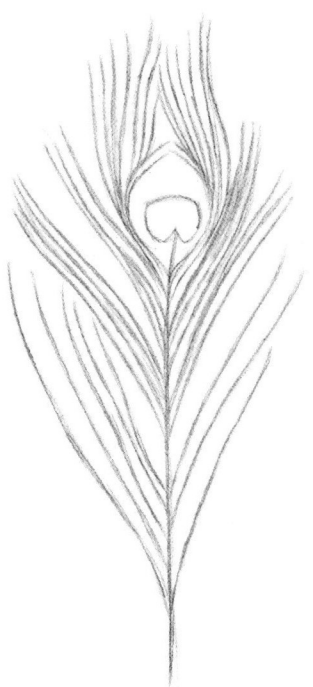

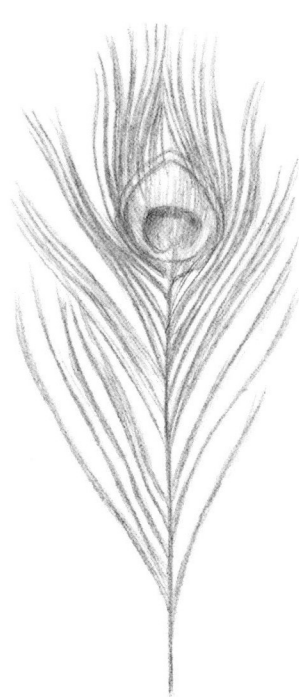

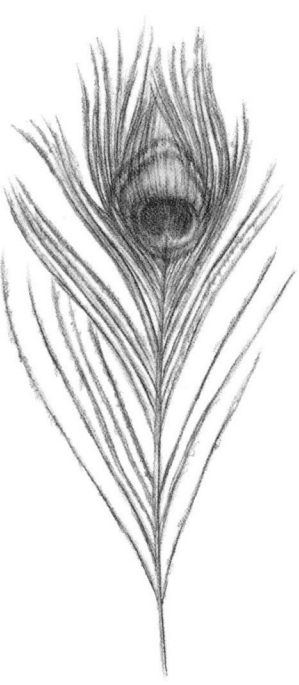

1 Start with lines drawn in the direction of the feather's growth that extend from a vertical line. For the eye of the peacock feather, draw a circle toward the top and lines that sweep past the eye around it.

2 Next, follow the pattern of the peacock feather and darken the center of the eye. Some of the feather fibers around the eye should remain fine and light to prevent the feather from appearing heavy.

3 Once all the dark areas have been drawn, use an eraser to lift out highlights in the eye.

Search for different types of feathers online or in nature,
and then draw them below.

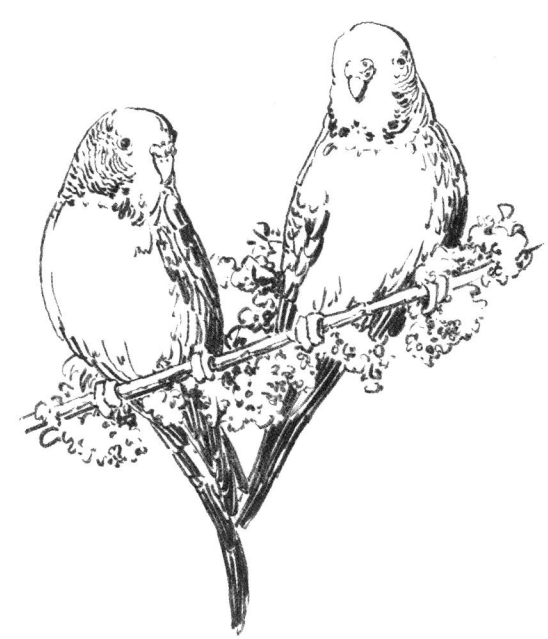

Chick

This chick is drawn using basic shapes and lines, including circles, ovals, and triangles.
Use basic shapes to complete the form, and then build out the form with shading.

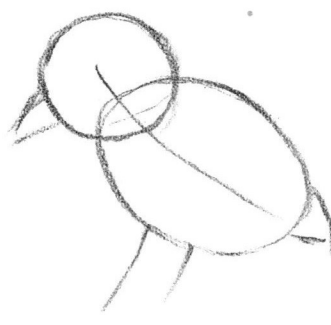

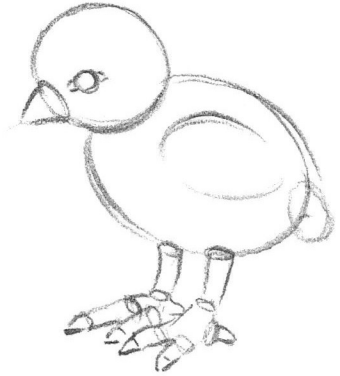

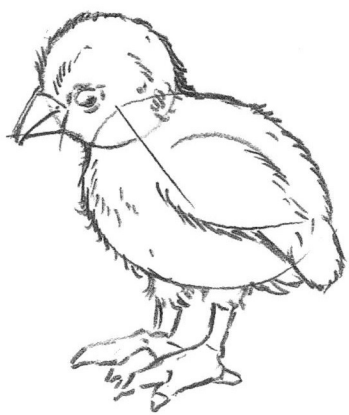

Basic Shape Start with simple circles, triangles, and ovals to draw the basic shapes of the chick, as well as the lines that connect these shapes.

Body Once the outlines are in place, work circles and triangles into spheres and cones to create depth and dimension.

Tracing When you connect the shapes and draw the construction lines, which will later be drawn over or erased, the image emerges in all its physicality.

Use the outlines below to master building out the form and details of baby chicks. Experiment with different pencils to see how they change the look and feel of each drawing.

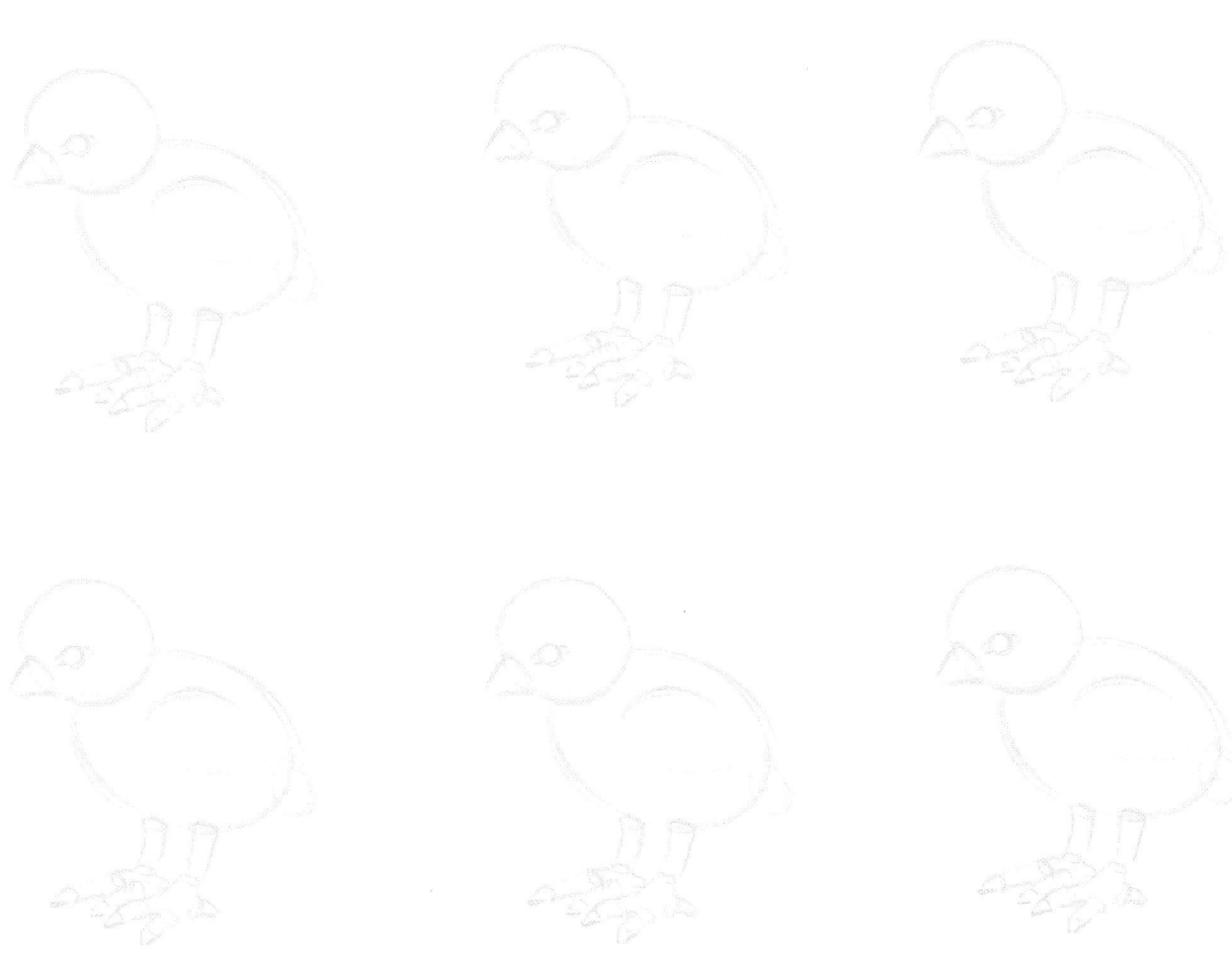

Hare

You need to carefully observe each animal you want to draw. For example, do you notice that the animal's ears aren't quite right in step one? They're too small and need to be improved.

1

In steps one and two, begin with ovals and circles, and block in the general shape, trying to catch the mood of the pose.

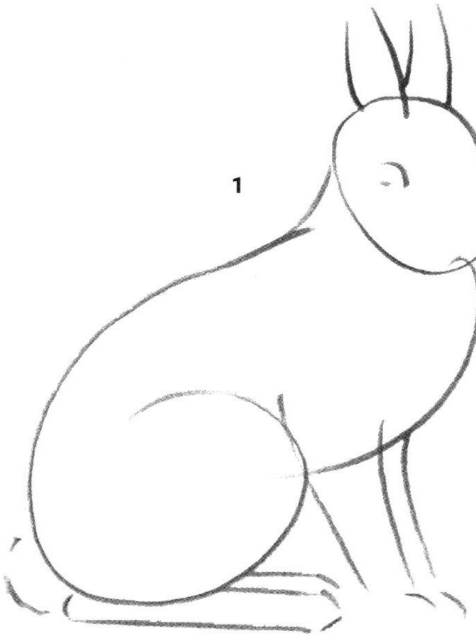

2

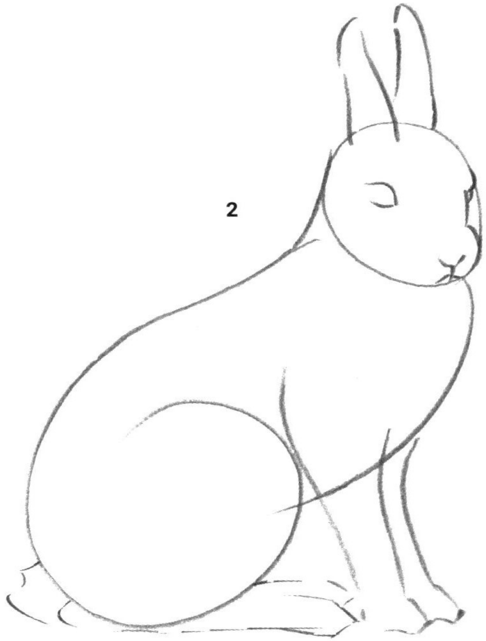

Once the basic structure is correct, begin to add the details.

3

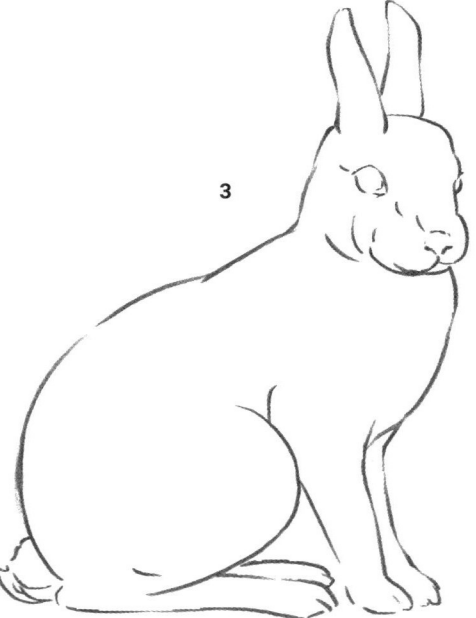

Complete the hare shown below, paying attention to the light source on its body and the highlight in its eyes.

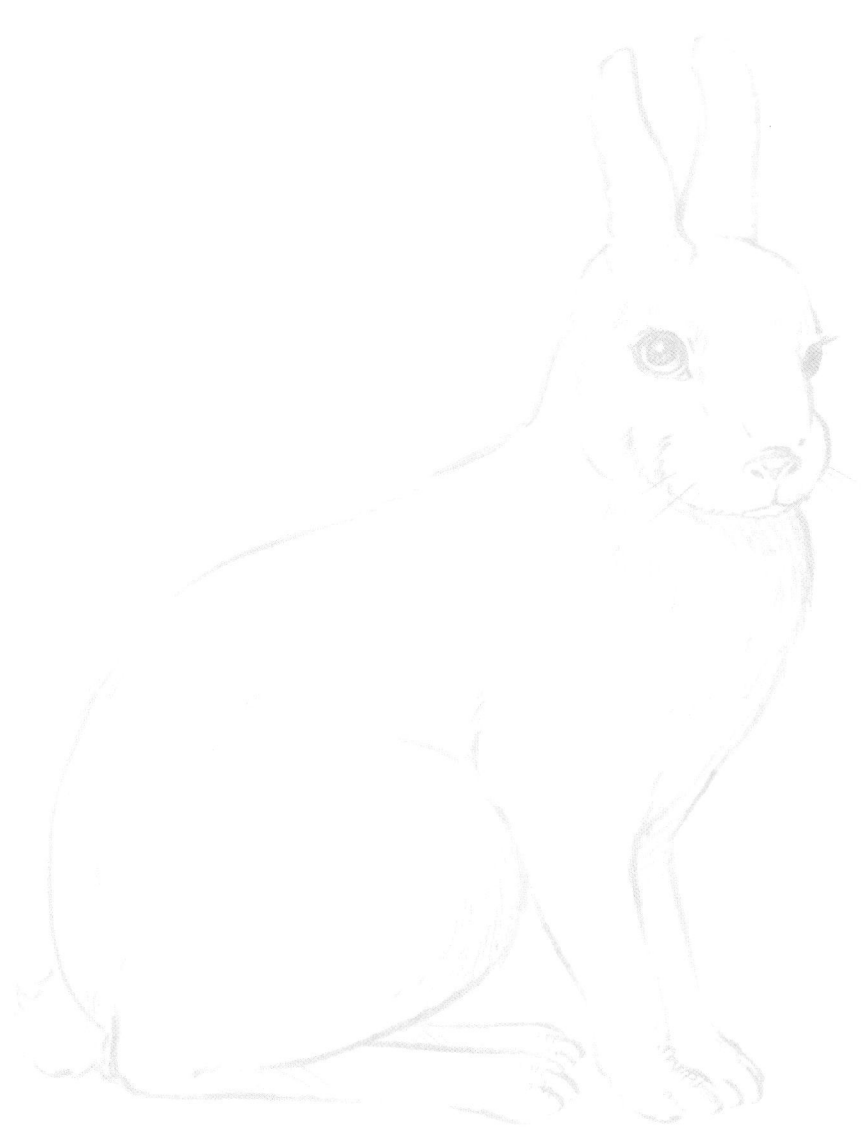

Rabbit

Rabbits differ from hares in appearance due to their rounder, more compact body size and softer, rounder ear shape. Rabbits live in packs and dig burrows, while hares prefer to live alone or in pairs.

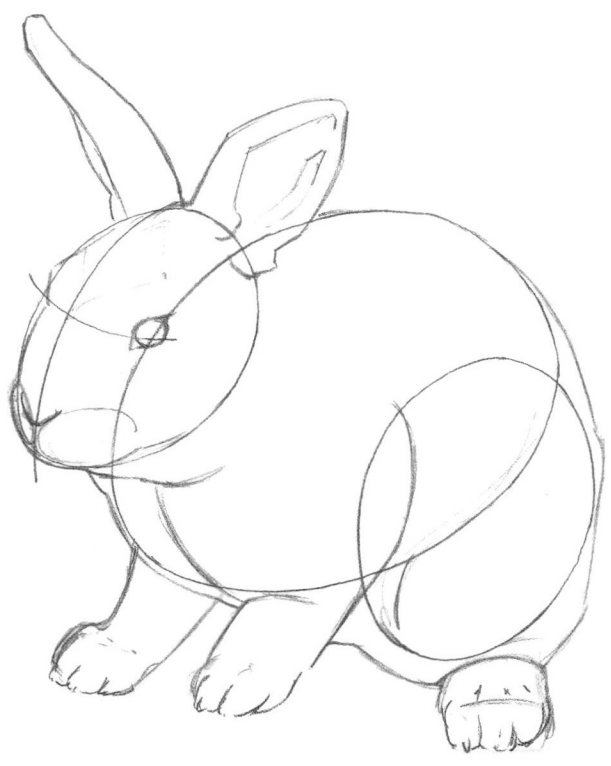

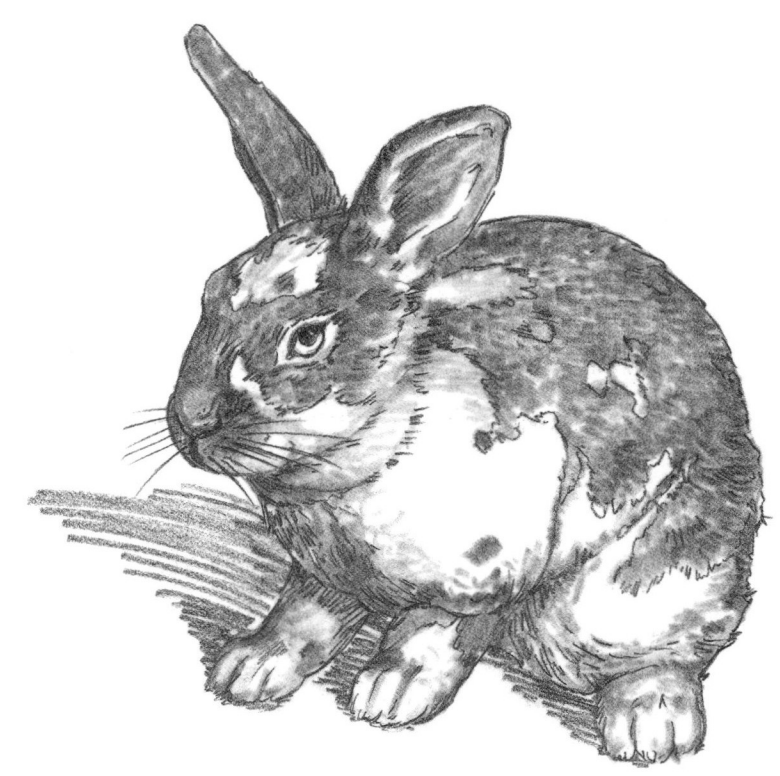

1 For the rabbit's head, body, and hind legs, draw three partially overlapping ovals. For the face, use two intersecting, curved lines. Using a few lines, join the ovals into a single outline and sketch the legs, paws, and ears. You can also position the eyes and nose using basic guidelines.

2 Begin to add the patches of dark fur with short, irregular strokes. Work on the eye and whiskers in detail. Also, add hatching to the underside and ears. Use a round-tip pencil and loose, soft strokes to draw the cast shadow.

Now it's your turn to give the rabbit a soft coat. Note how the quick, light strokes make the rabbit's fur appear light and fluffy.

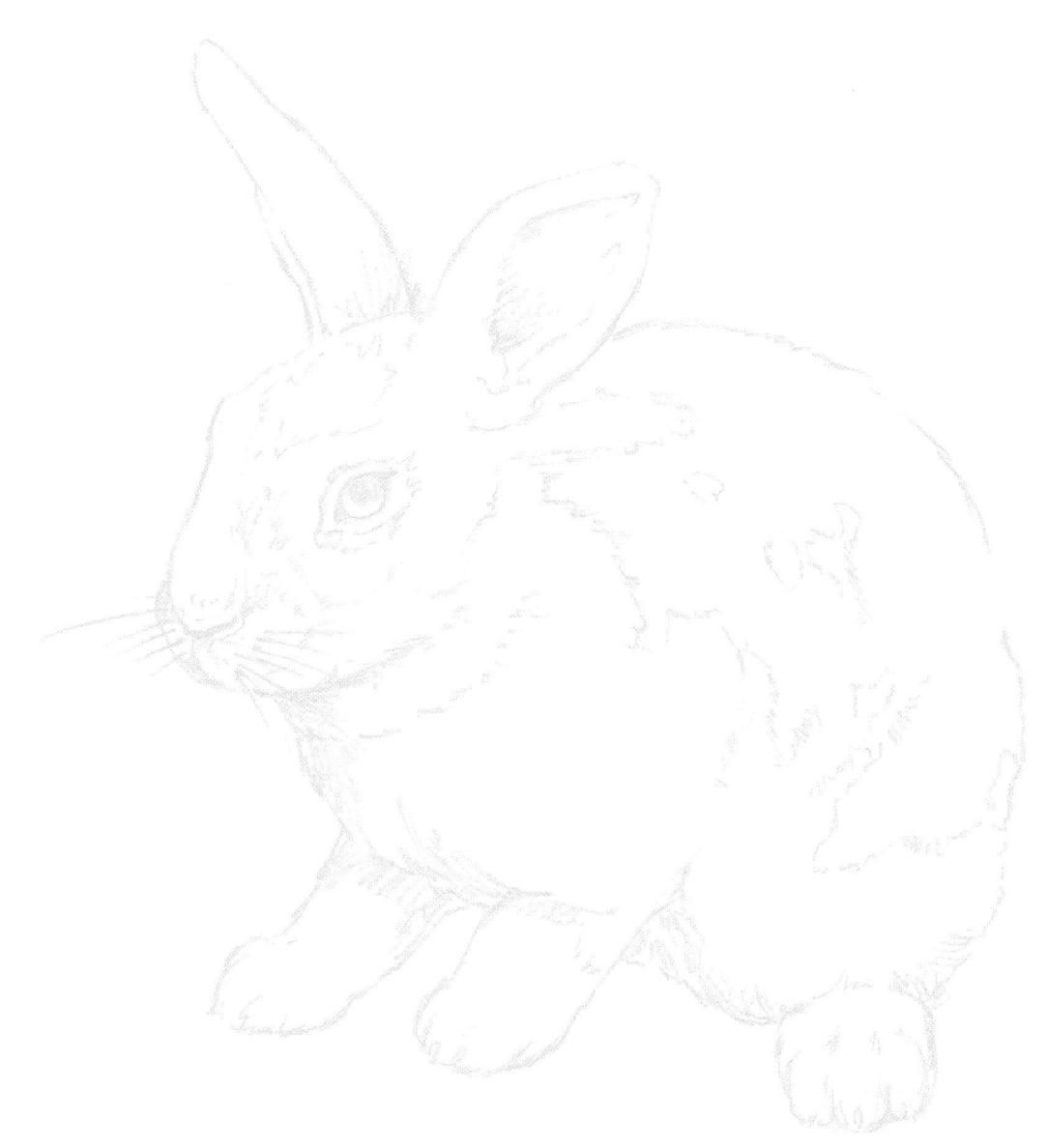

Giant Panda

A panda is easy to draw if you work step by step, starting with circles for the head and body. Then add ovals for the arms, legs, and paws, as well as details like the eyes, nose, and bamboo leaves. Using soft, short strokes, this bear's fur looks thick and cuddly.

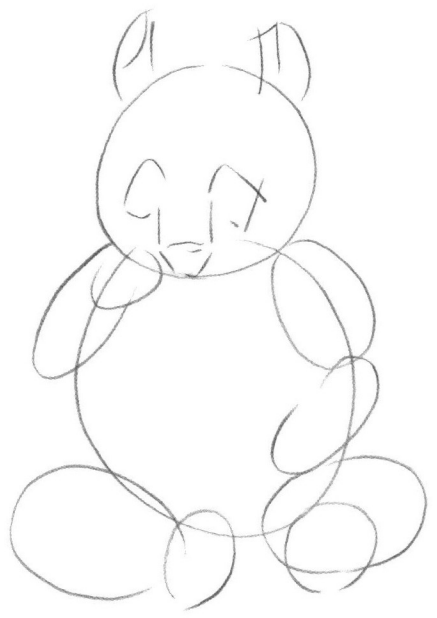 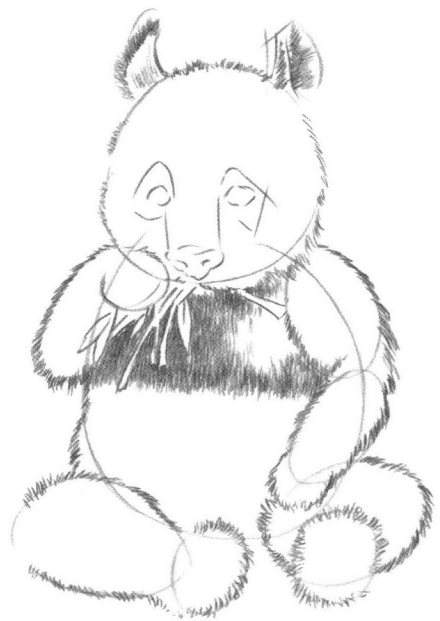 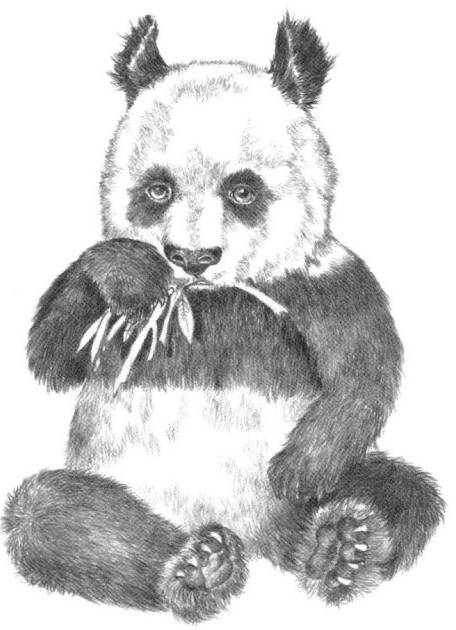

1 Draw a circle for the head and a larger oval for the belly. Use smaller ovals for the legs, upper and lower arms, and feet. A few strokes define the position of the eyes, ears, and nose.

2 Sketch the eyes, nose, and bamboo branch. Using short, soft strokes, cover the panda with fur. Using an HB pencil, draw the dark fur on the chest, following the direction of fur growth.

3 Continue to draw the fur with soft, short strokes. Don't worry about shading the fur evenly. Light and dark areas will add shape to the form. Complete the feet, claws, nose, and eyes.

Shade in the darkest areas of the fur. Then soften the lines with a blending stump. Draw a few contours that reveal the bear's stocky shape.

Wolf

The wolf has a straight back and lets its tail hang when walking. It has a relatively large head with a broad forehead, a long muzzle, and short, rounded ears that point forward. Its eyes are set close together and are slightly slanted.

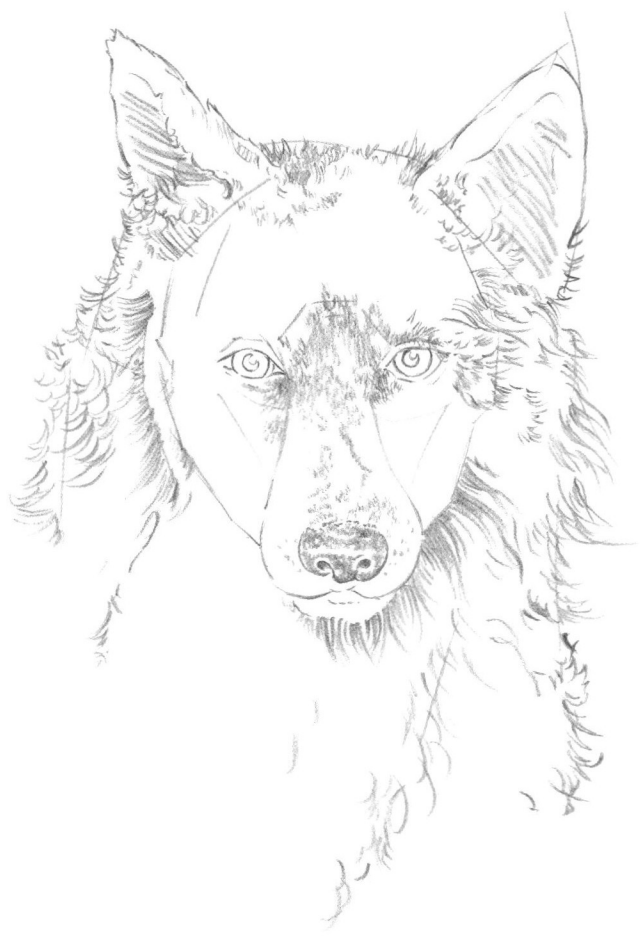

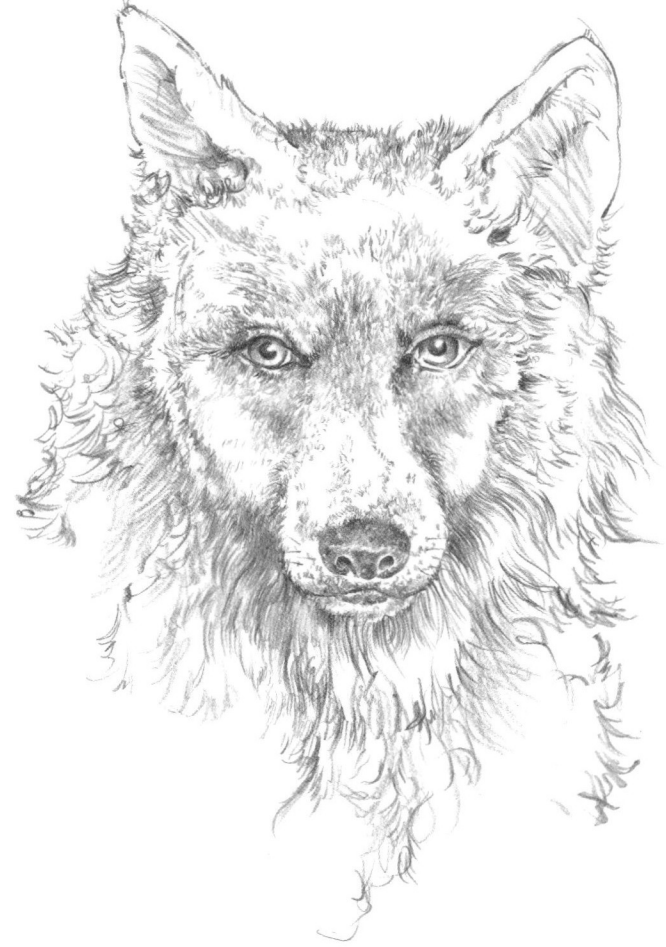

1 Start the hatching with the darkest tones in areas like the inside of the ears or under the muzzle. Create the fur using different shades of gray and different strokes and lines to render the fur as realistically as possible.

2 Detail the wolf's fur and face, including the eyes and nose. Leave some areas on the ears, forehead, and front of the snout white. Lift out light reflections with a kneaded eraser.

Draw a wolf using the outline below. Carefully develop
the eyes and facial features.

Polar Bear

With an oval-shaped body, rounded ears, and angular snout, the polar bear makes for a good beginning drawing project. Start with broad, rounded shapes to block in this bear's massive frame. Then develop the details as you go.

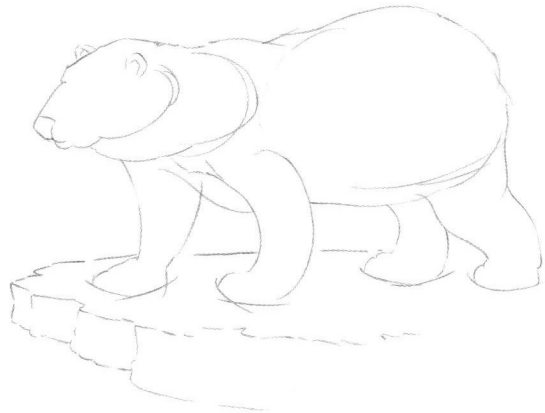

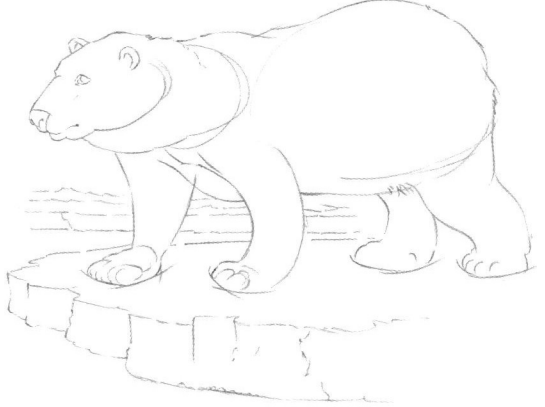

1 Sketch the outlines of the body, head, and legs, paying careful attention to proportions. Draw a few lines to indicate the length of the neck and two quick strokes for the chest. Notice that the head is slightly lower than the rear, and that the front legs curve slightly inward.

2 Add the ears with two semi-circles and block in the squarish nose. Sketch the thick ice floe beneath the bear's feet. Start with an irregular half-oval and then draw a matching line beneath it, connecting the top and the base with vertical lines.

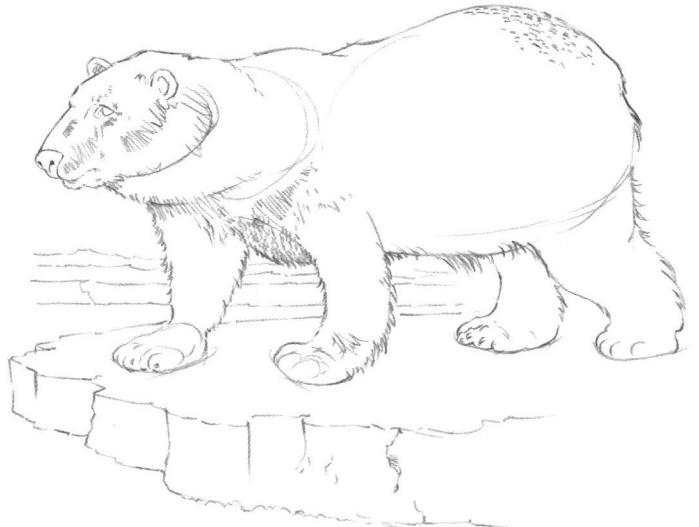

3 Place the eye and begin building the feet with circular strokes. To suggest the mass of ice in the background, add four broken horizontal lines behind the ice floe.

Apply shading to the bear with short strokes that follow the direction
of hair growth. Use an HB pencil to complete the ice floe
and indicate the water.

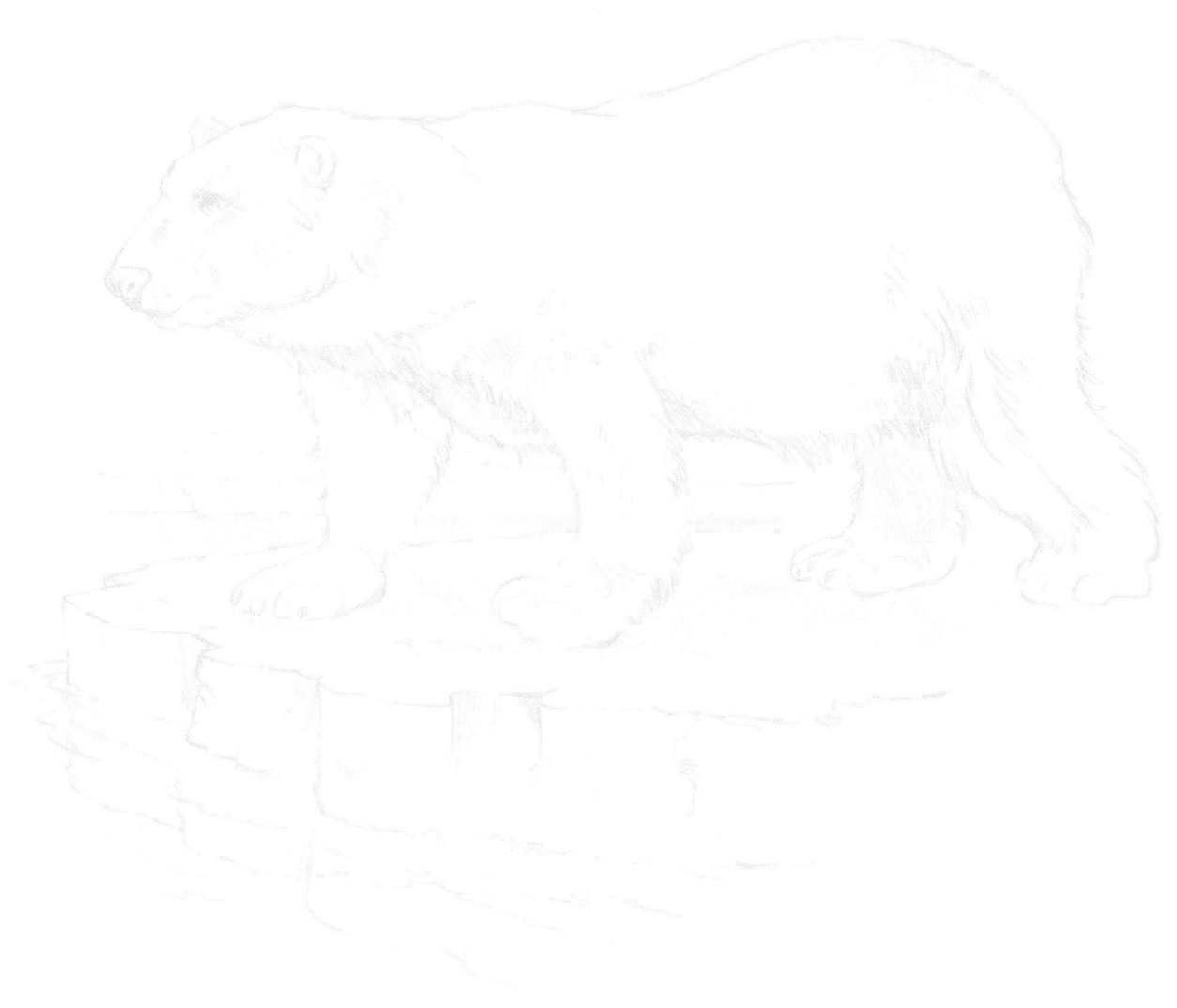

Horse in Profile

In the early stages of your drawing, it's important to establish accurate proportions; you don't want to make major adjustments after you've started adding detail and shading. To get the proportions as precise as possible, use plenty of guidelines to block in the basic shapes. Learning this process of creating and working within guidelines will help you work successfully from your own references.

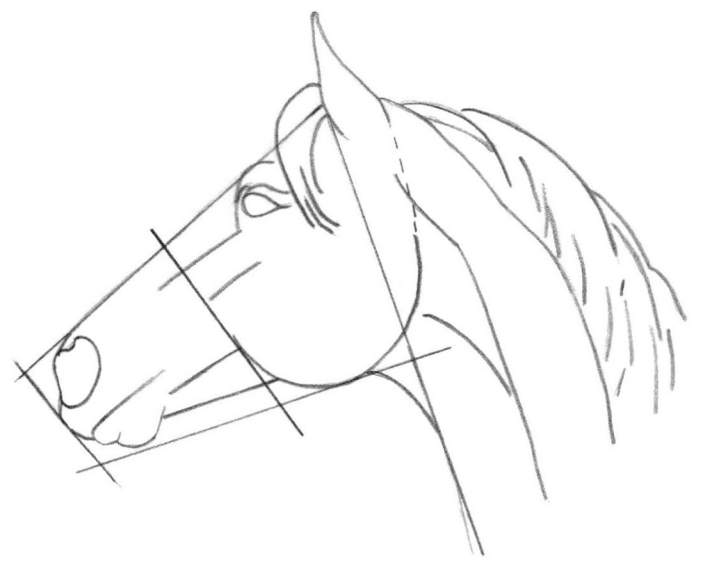

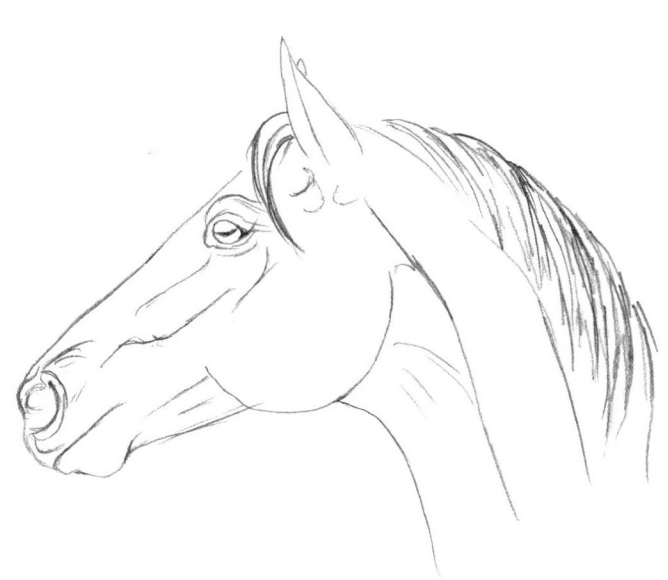

1 Use an HB pencil and light pressure to block in the basic shape of the horse's head. Use quick, diagonal strokes to indicate the muzzle, ear, and back of the head. Then divide the head vertically at the midpoint. This will provide a reference for adding the jawline.

2 Working within the guidelines, begin refining the neck, muzzle, and jaw. Carefully place the eye and nostril; then indicate the line of the mouth. Roughly indicate the curve of the jaw with lines that extend to the base of the ears. Then add a few curves to suggest the form of the neck.

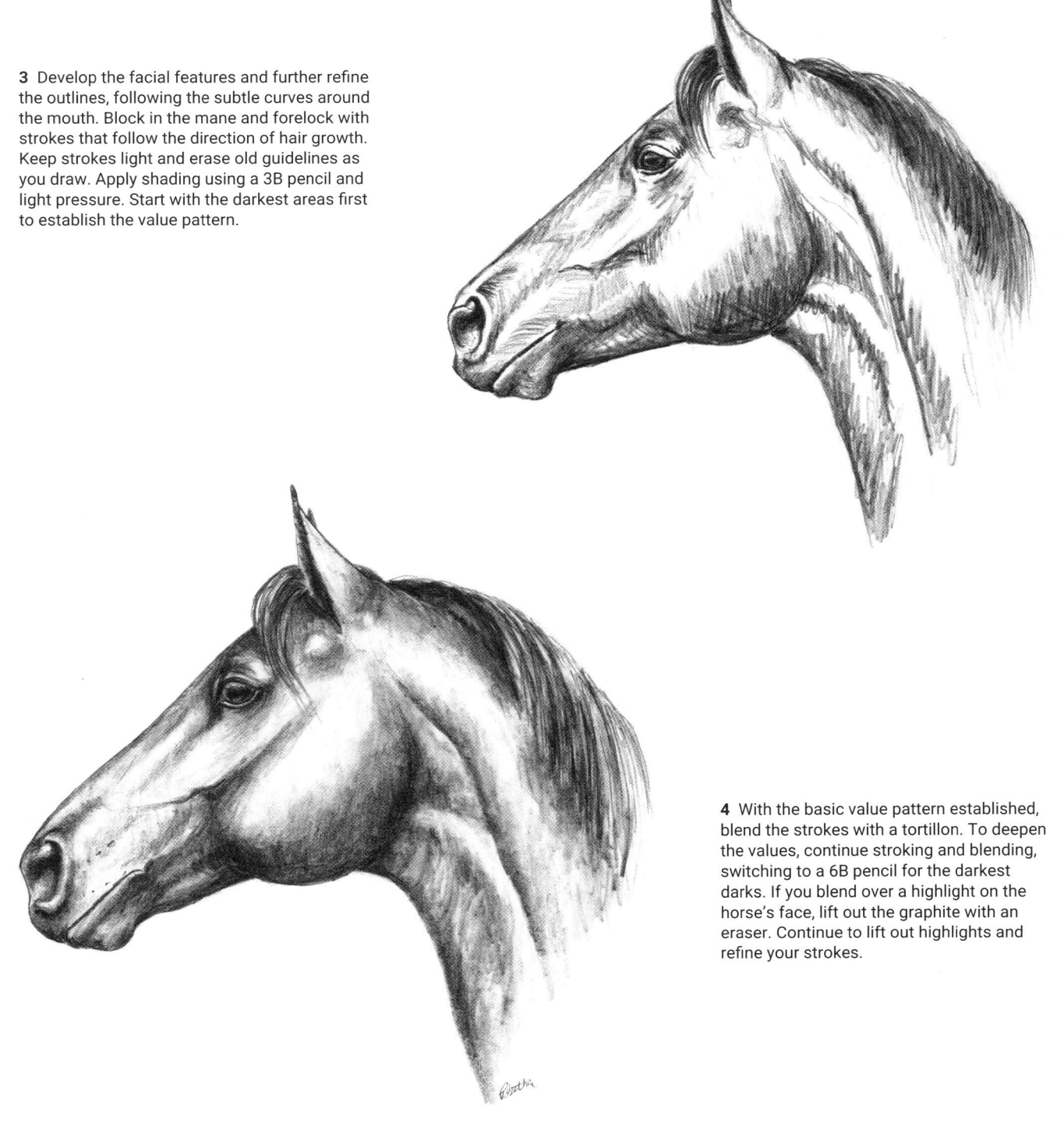

3 Develop the facial features and further refine the outlines, following the subtle curves around the mouth. Block in the mane and forelock with strokes that follow the direction of hair growth. Keep strokes light and erase old guidelines as you draw. Apply shading using a 3B pencil and light pressure. Start with the darkest areas first to establish the value pattern.

4 With the basic value pattern established, blend the strokes with a tortillon. To deepen the values, continue stroking and blending, switching to a 6B pencil for the darkest darks. If you blend over a highlight on the horse's face, lift out the graphite with an eraser. Continue to lift out highlights and refine your strokes.

Arabian

The Arabian is a high-spirited horse with a flamboyant tail carriage and distinctive dished profile. Though relatively small in stature, this breed is known for its stamina, graceful build, intelligence, and energy. Try to capture the Arabian's slender physique and high spirit in your drawing.

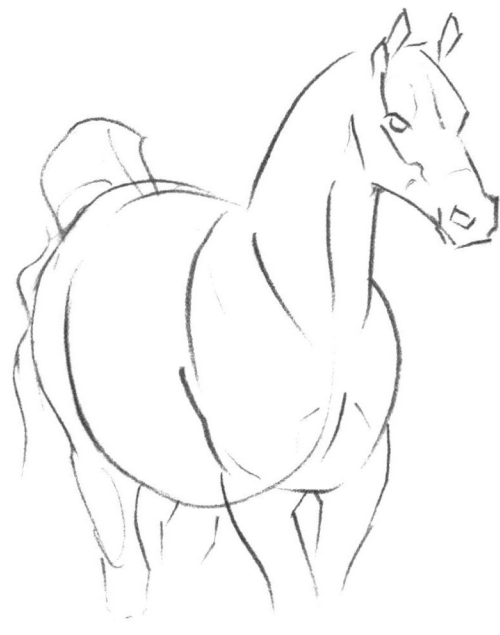

1 Using an HB pencil, draw an oval for the body at a slight angle to indicate that it is foreshortened. When blocking in the head, take care to stress the concave nose, large nostrils, and small muzzle.

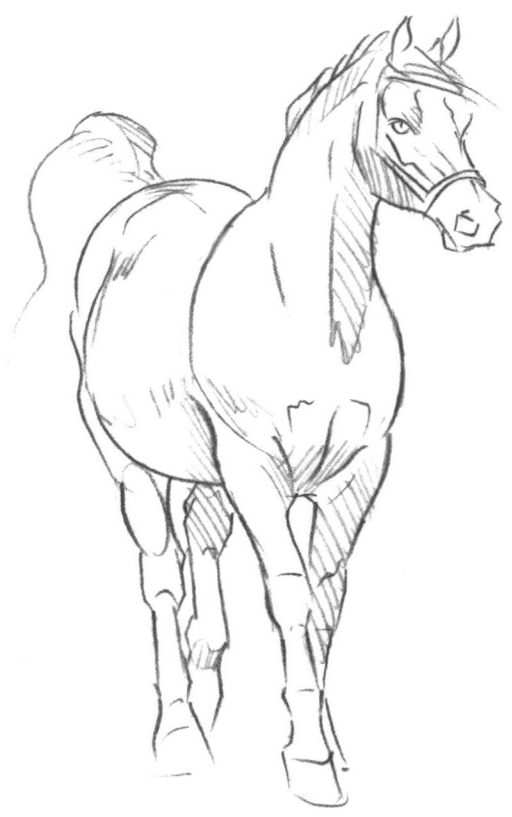

2 As you start shading, keep the lines for the tail loose and free. Accent the graceful arch of the neck.

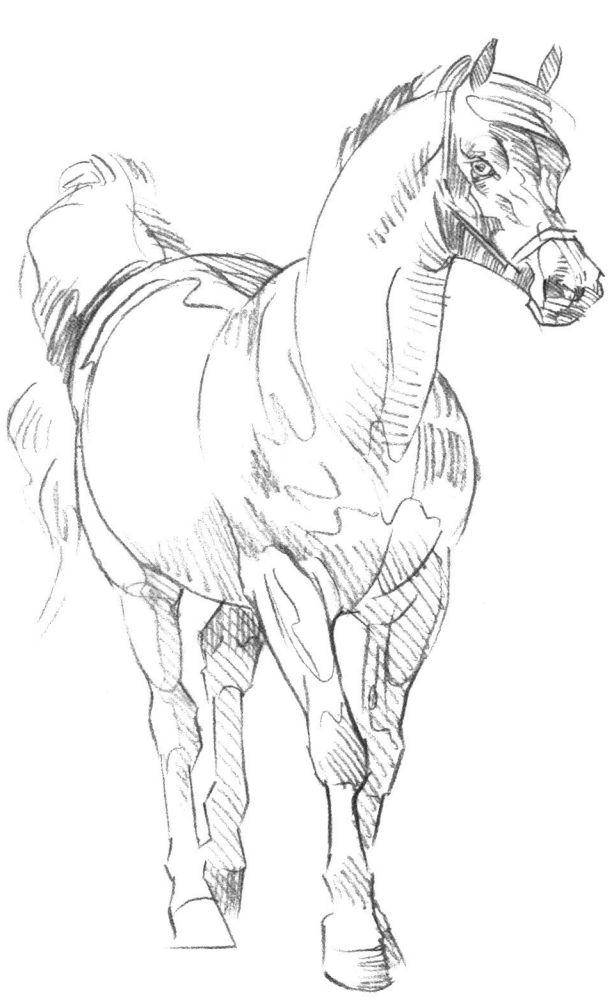

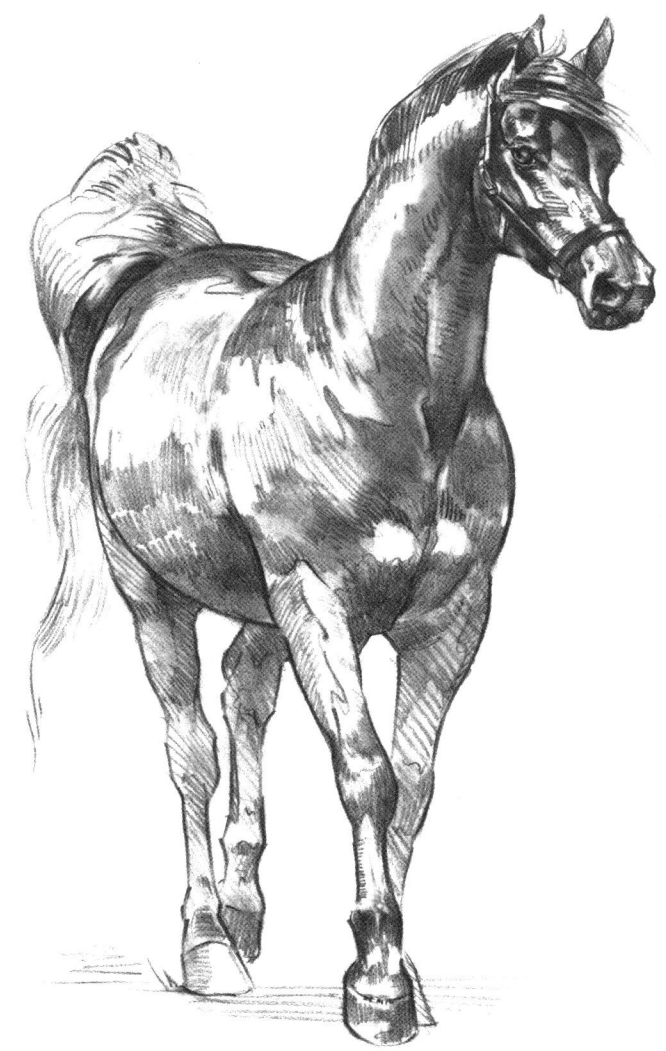

3 Be sure to emphasize this horse's narrow chest and face to convey its more delicate build. Build up values over the face and body, delineating areas of highlight.

4 Refine your shading with a soft lead pencil and blending stump, leaving large areas of white for the highlights. These highlights show the shine of the horse's coat and indicate the direction of the light source.

Cat Fur

Every cat breed has its own unique fur—long or short, soft or thick, striped or solid. You can easily depict different fur types using the techniques shown here. And you don't have to draw every hair individually.

Solid-colored fur

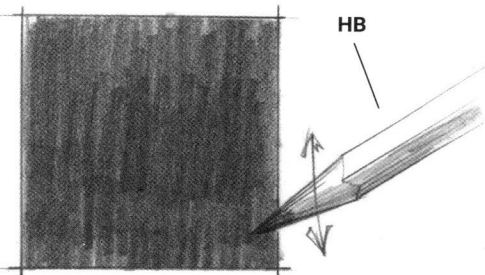

1 Cover the surface evenly with the side of an HB pencil and vertical strokes. Apply several coats.

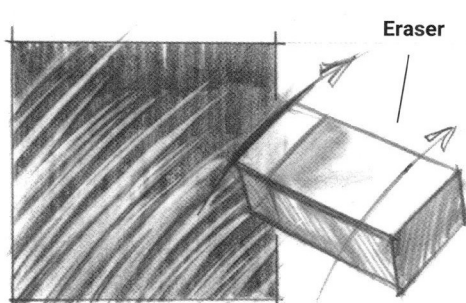

2 Erase individual light hairs in the direction of hair growth. Lift the eraser at the end to create a nice hair tip.

Striped fur

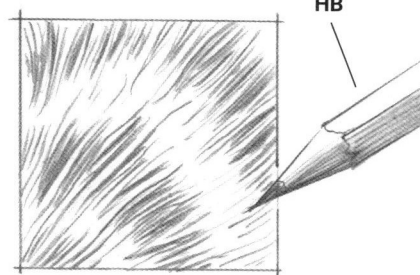

1 Using an HB pencil (tip and sides), first draw the dark fur areas.

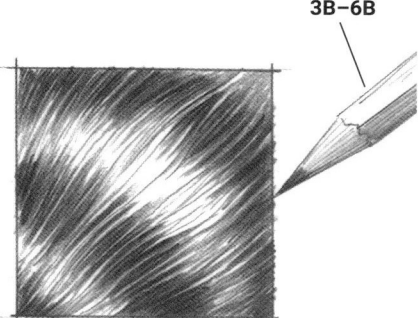

2 Work out the structure and details with pencils between 3B and 6B; soften any harsh transitions with the blending stump.

Thick fur

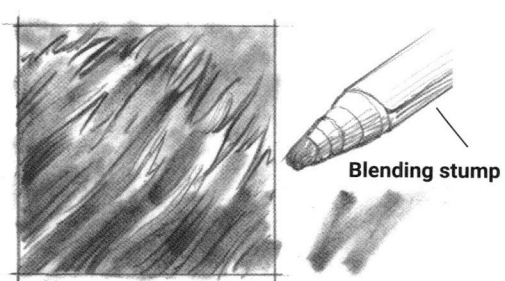

1 Apply thin lines with an HB pencil; then smudge some lines with a blending stump.

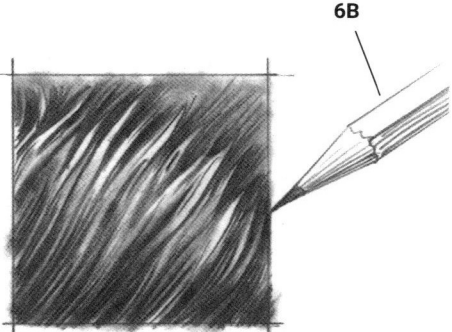

2 Using a sharp 6B pencil, rework the fur texture in the direction of hair growth. Lift out highlights with an eraser.

Use the boxes below to practice drawing cat fur using different types of pencils and techniques. Use a kneaded eraser to lift out highlights to give the fur depth and dimension.

Persian Cat

Persians are stocky cats with long, silky hair. They have a large, round face with a short nose and small ears. To capture the unique texture of the Angora coat, you need to work evenly and carefully. Make sure to draw the pencil strokes in the direction of the fur growth. Each stroke should follow the natural contours of the face so the fur looks natural and not stiff.

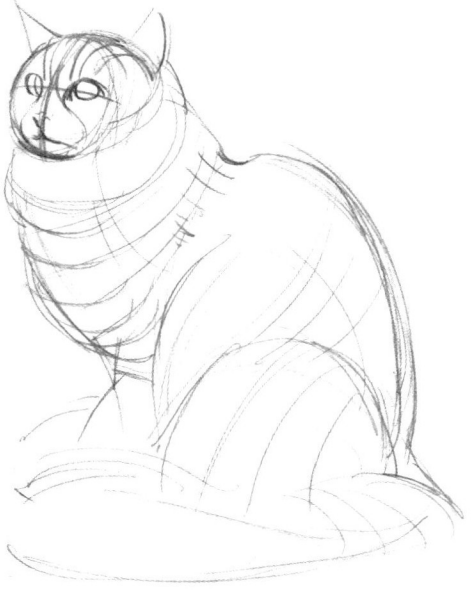

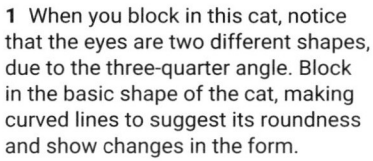

Notice how the dark background creates the shape of the light-colored fur on the cat's chest and tail.

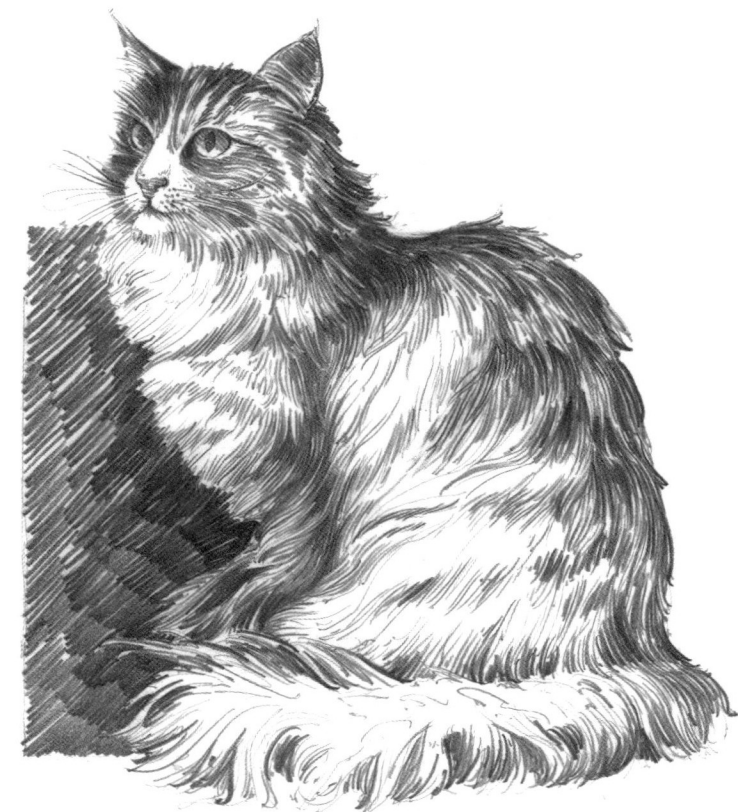

1 When you block in this cat, notice that the eyes are two different shapes, due to the three-quarter angle. Block in the basic shape of the cat, making curved lines to suggest its roundness and show changes in the form.

2 Use uniform pencil strokes to indicate the layers of fur around the head, chest, and back. The minimal shading in the white areas on the cat's chest and side reflect where the light strikes the coat. The middle values are shown in the fur along the left side of the cat's face and left ear. Use a 4B or 6B pencil for darker strokes along the backbone, neck, right side of the face, and parts of the tail.

Use 2B and 4B pencils to bring out the thick texture of the fur.
Remember to draw lines in the direction of fur growth.

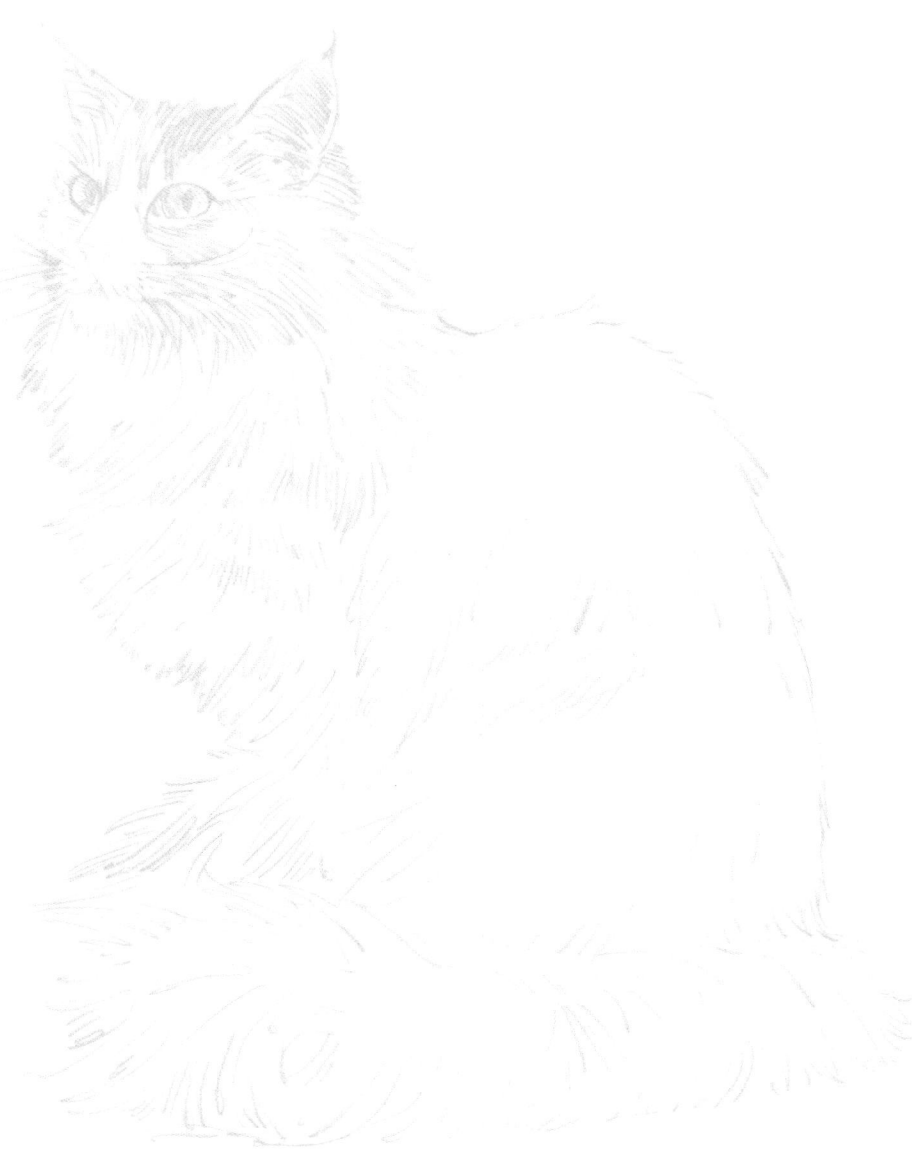

Kitten

In this scene, the ball of yarn in which the kitten's paws are tangled is intended to be the focal point. Can you spot all the tricks used to achieve this? Most notably, the yarn is lifted out with an eraser inside the dark background.

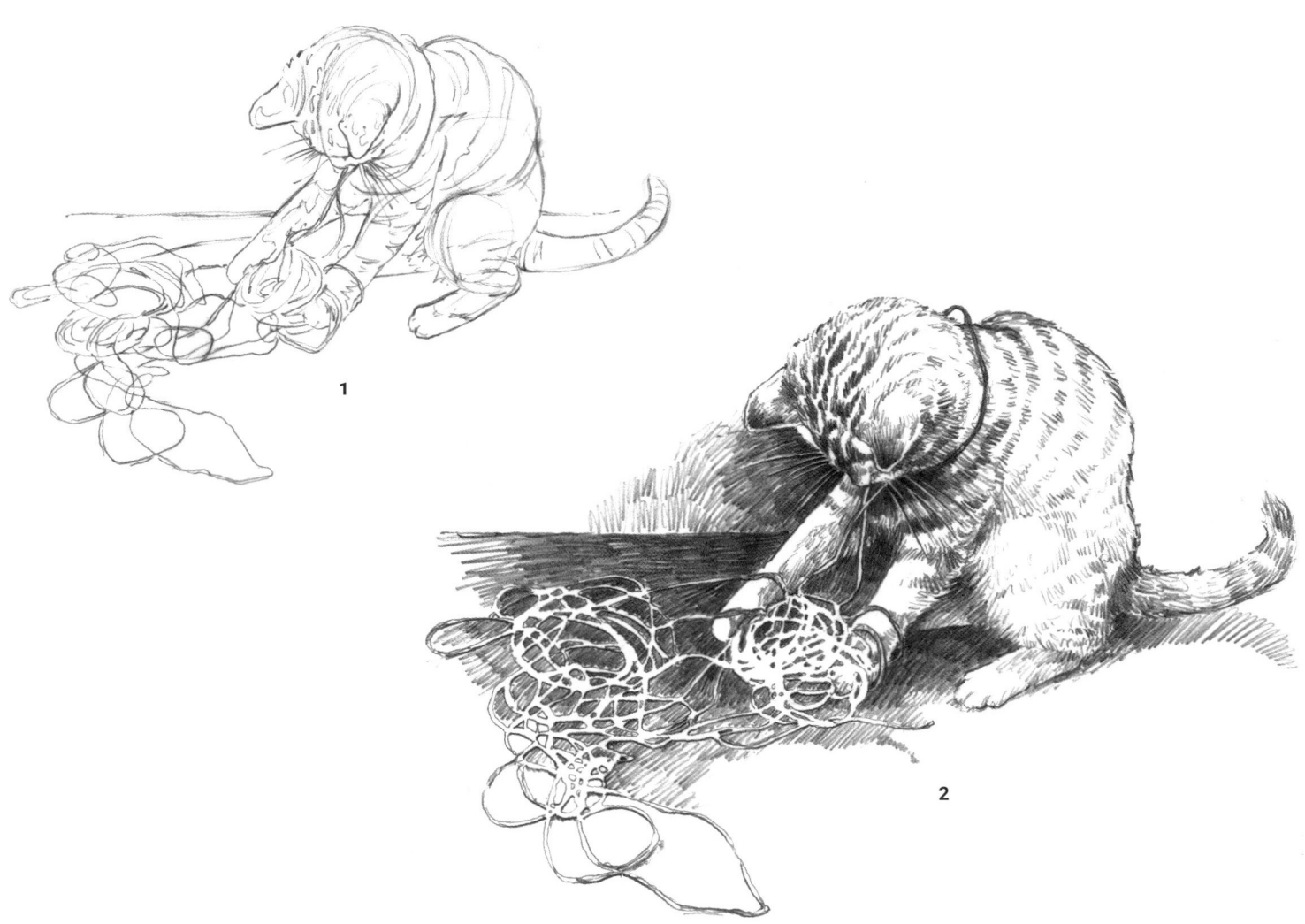

Use pencils of varying hardness or a fine-line marker to enhance the drawing. The cat has short fur, and the string is partially cut out in white.

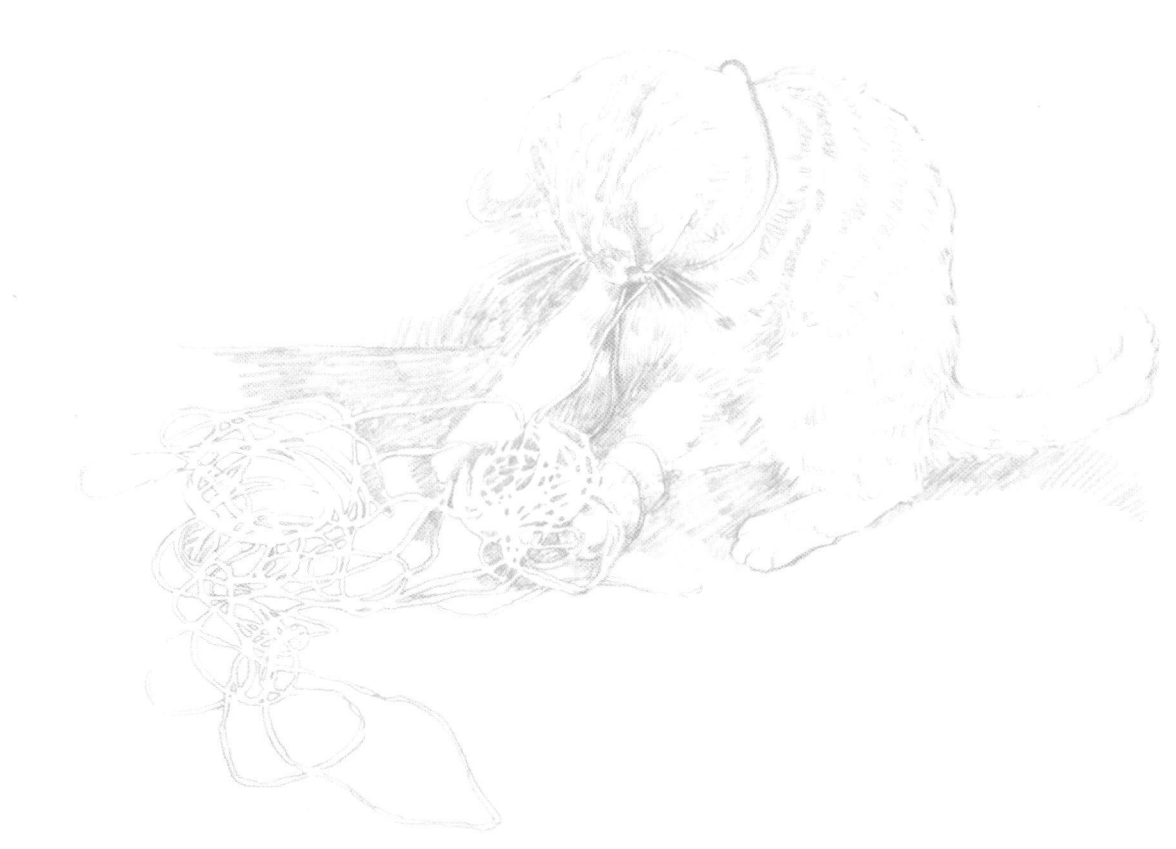

Climbing Kitten

Cats love to climb, although this kitten has found itself in a precarious situation! Note that kittens have round, barrel-shaped bodies, whereas adult cats have long, lanky bodies. Follow the steps to draw this kitten.

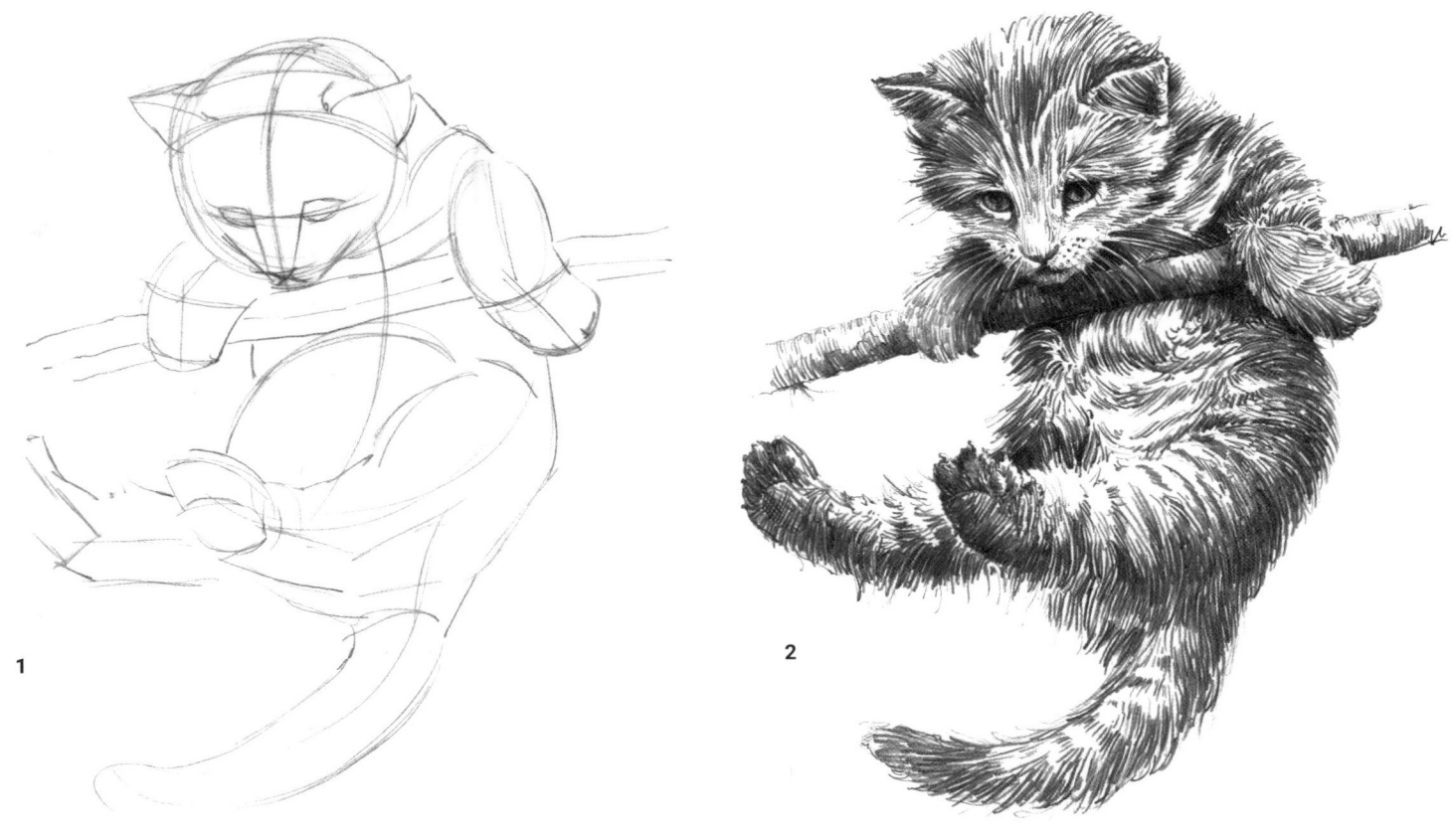

1

2

Draw the cat's long, wiry fur.
Increase shading of the fur in darker areas.

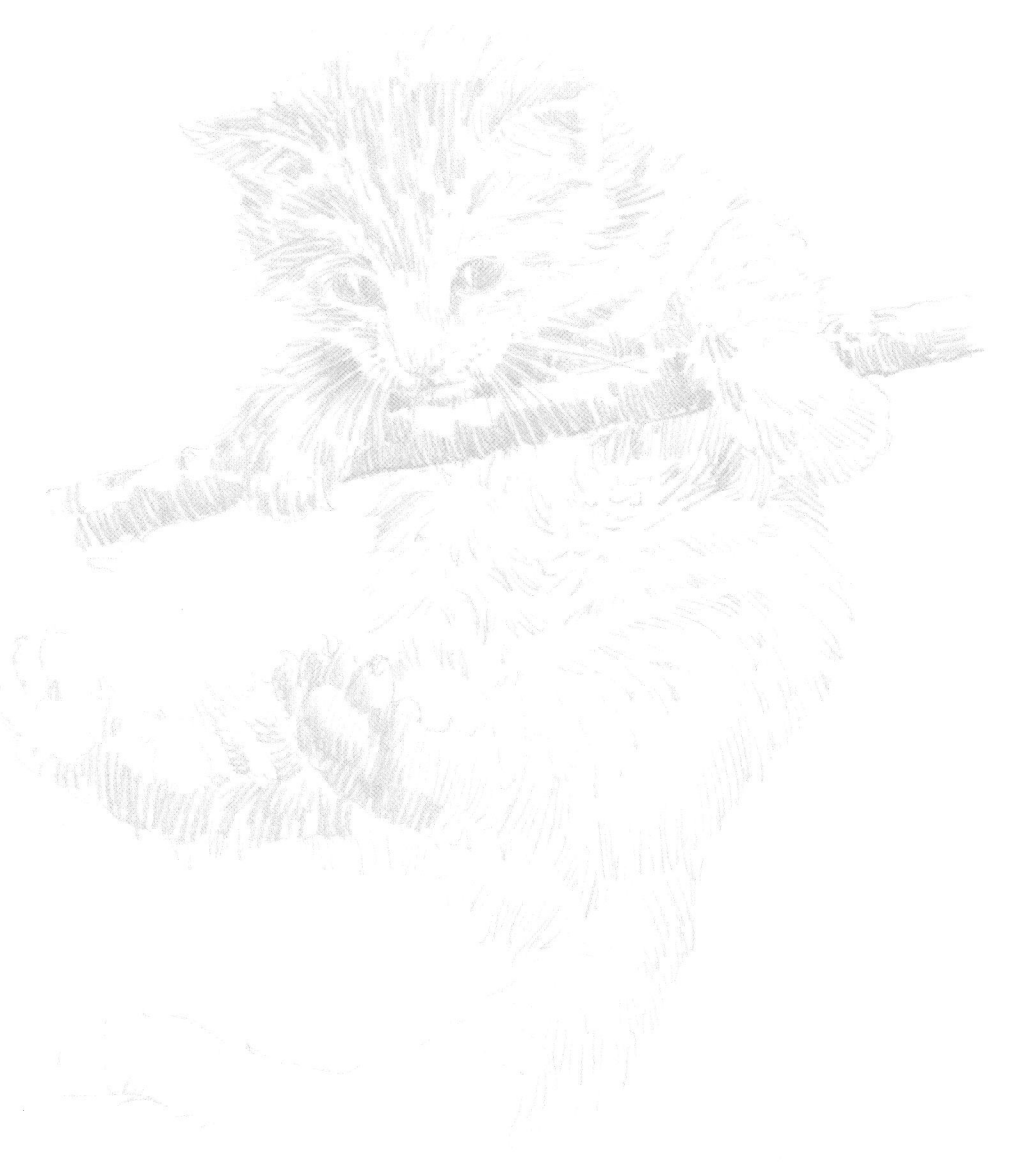

Dog in Profile

Study the dog carefully before drawing, and make an effort to accurately capture its distinctive features. Is its muzzle pointed or rounded? Is its hair long and soft or short and smooth? When you begin drawing, approach your subject gradually.

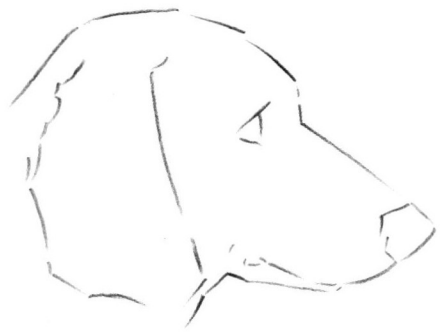

1 Lightly sketch the basic outline and structure of the head. Use the side of an HB pencil to draw the corners.

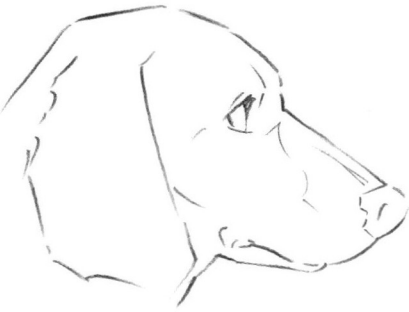

2 Indicate the details of the face and the nose with a few basic lines.

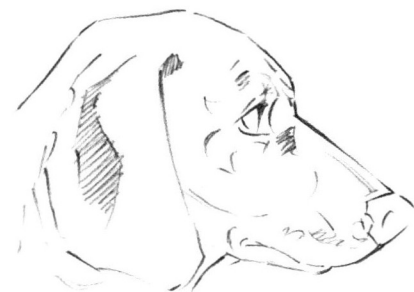

3 Apply shading to define the shape using the rounded tip and the broad side of an HB pencil.

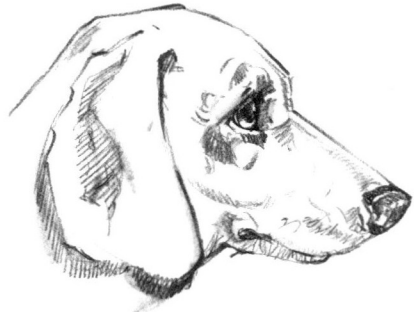

4 Use the tip and broad side of a sharpened pencil to draw individual sections of hair, gradually thickening the hatching. Use a well-sharpened 2B pencil for the darkest areas.

Great Danes are elegant in appearance and have a distinctive head.
Use HB, 4B, and 6B pencils to fill in the outline below.

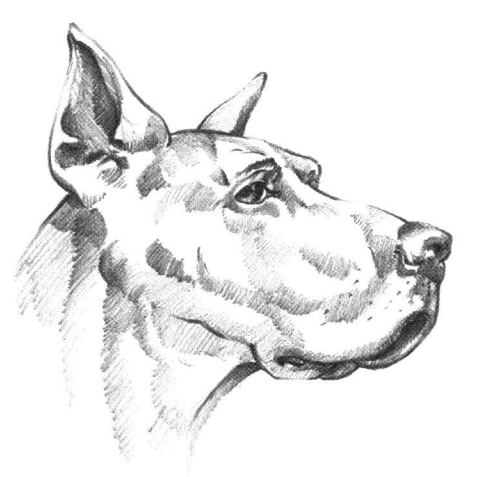

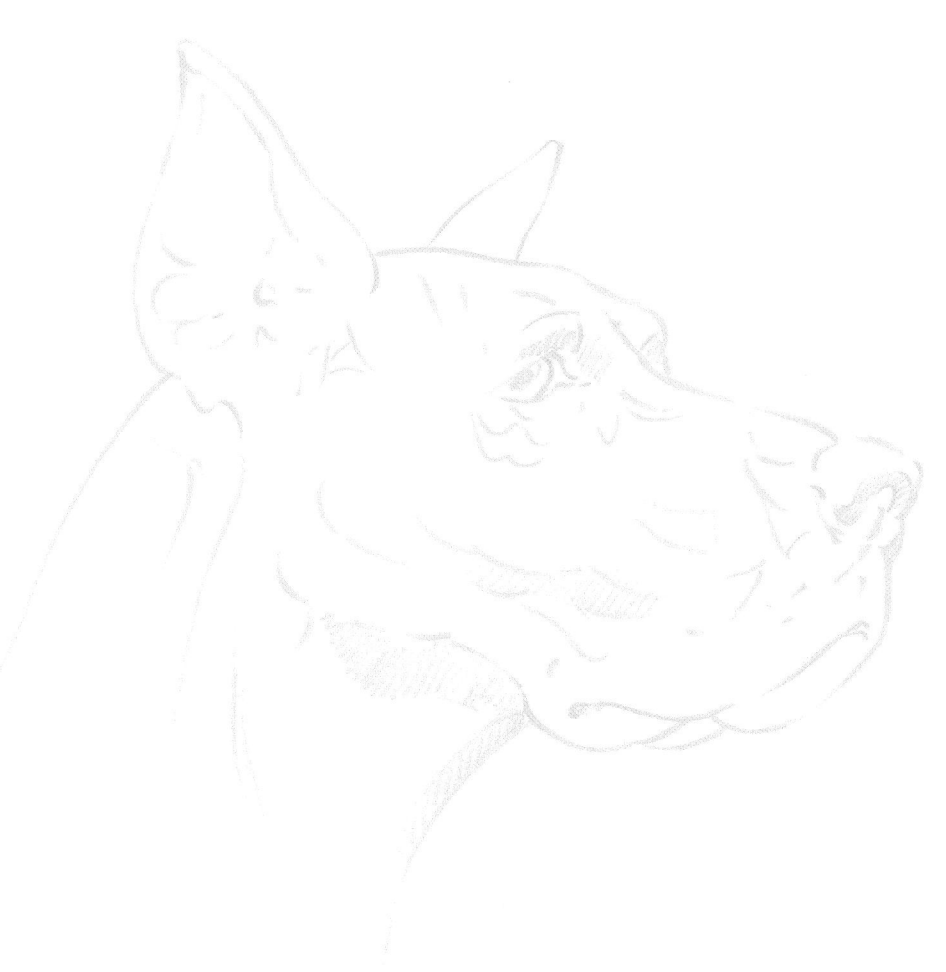

Dog Eyes

To create an expressive dog portrait, the eyes must be drawn accurately. It helps if you practice drawing dog eyes consistently, as they are an element that determines how realistic your drawing will be. Don't forget to leave white speck for the highlight.

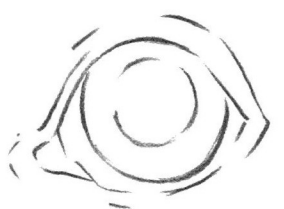

1

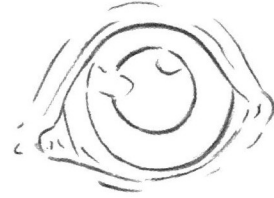

2

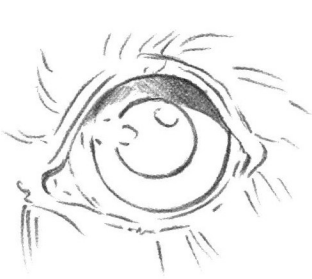

3

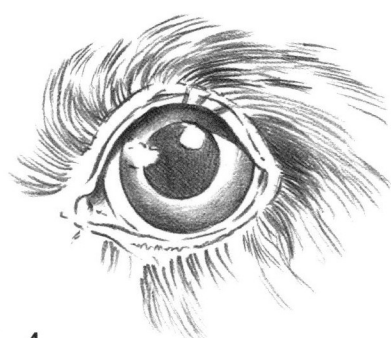

4

Give this dog expressive eyes and fill in its fur using some
of the techniques you've learned so far.

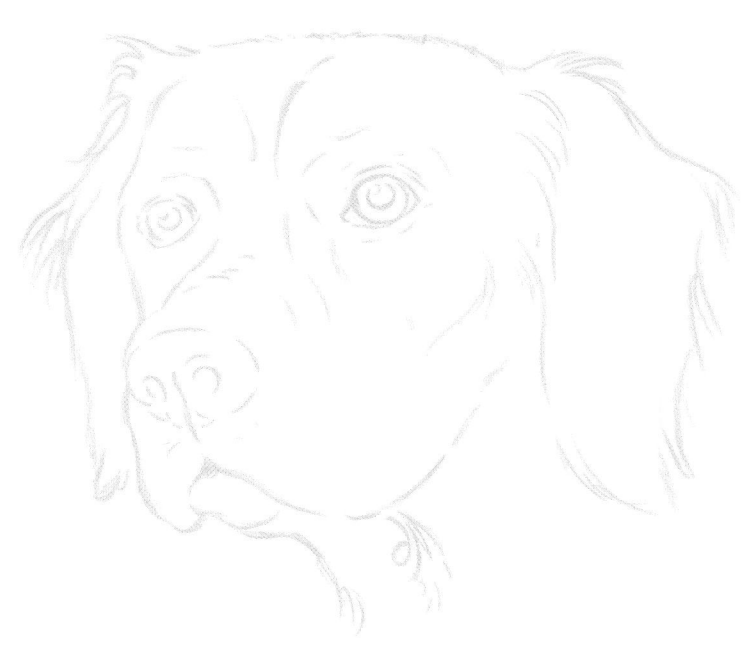

Golden Retriever

This dog breed is a true family pet. Their good nature is evident in their eyes, and their long, silky coat is perfect for petting and cuddling.

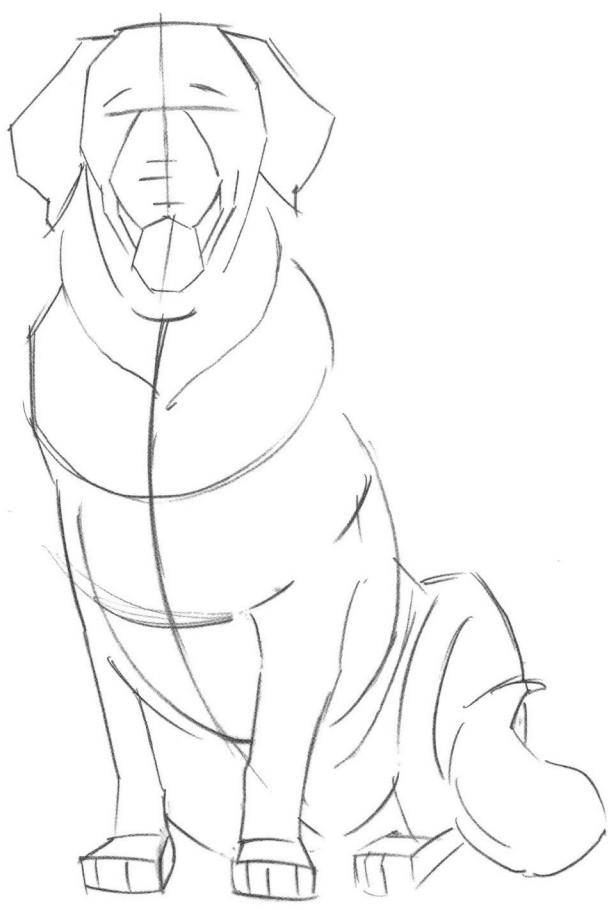

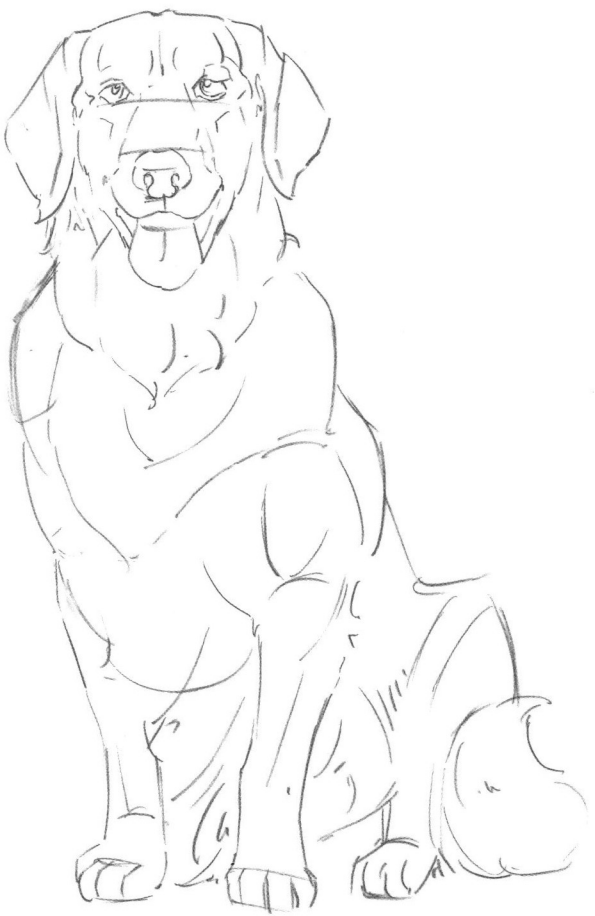

1 Use soft, sweeping lines to capture the fullness of this dog. Draw guidelines for the face: a line for the eyes in the upper third and a line for the nose in the middle. Use blocky shapes for the paws.

2 Next, position the facial features using the guidelines. Draw the soft fur, marking its drape with V-shaped guidelines. Erase any old sketch lines as you draw.

Use the outline below to practice drawing the golden retriever.

Drawing from a Photograph

Animals are wonderful subjects for drawing, especially when drawing from photos. If you're taking the photos yourself, try to capture a moment when the animal is making a characteristic movement, and take as many shots of the same animal as possible. Capturing an animal's distinctive personality isn't always easy, but the wait is always worth it!

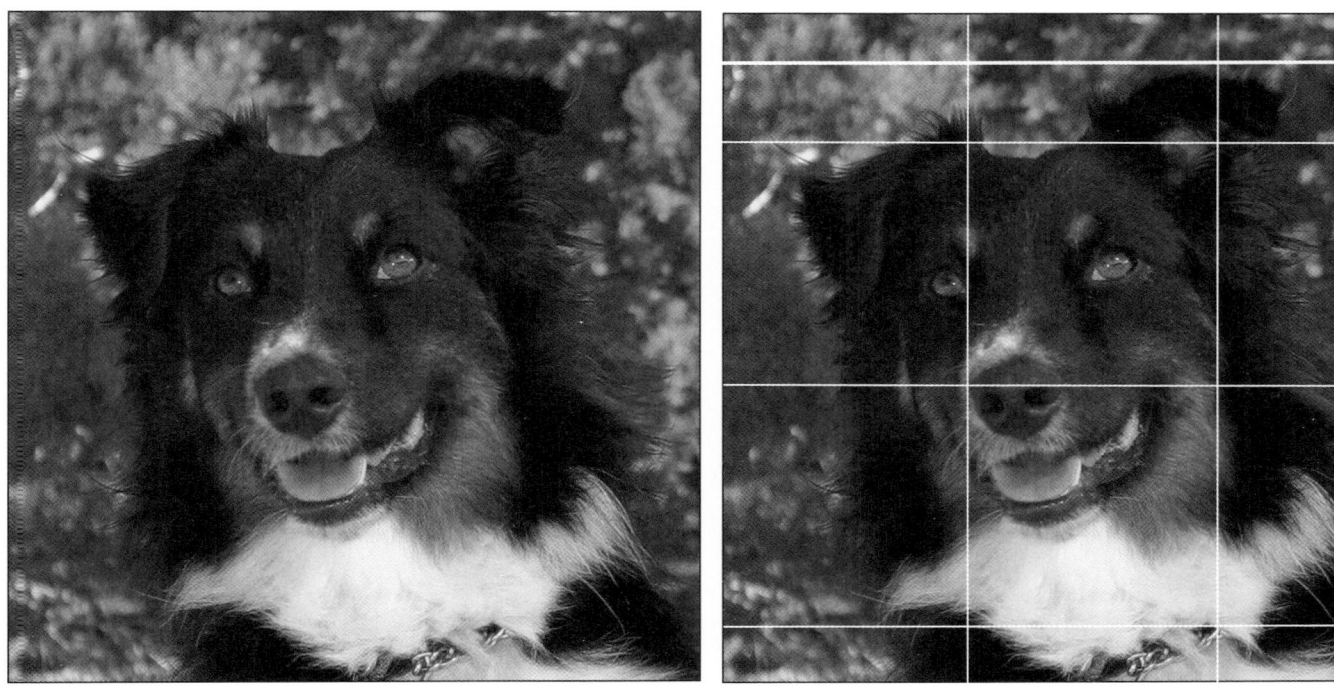

Grid Method Using grid lines as a guide, you can position your subject's facial features precisely. Draw the grid very lightly so it can be easily erased once the subject is fully drawn.

Transfer the outline of the dog's head to this grid
and then complete the portrait.

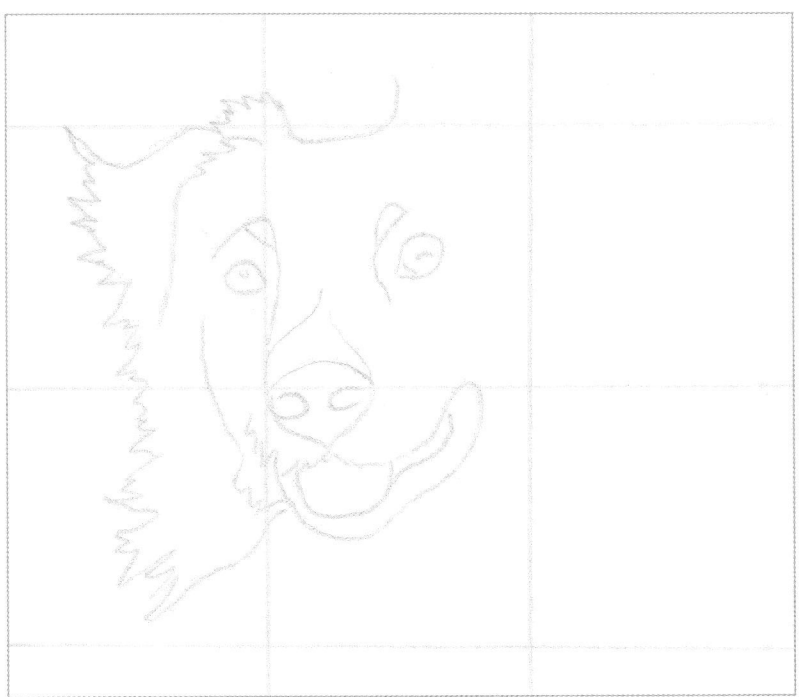

Adult Facial Proportions

If you want to draw a portrait, it's important to know how to arrange and place the facial features in relation to one another. Understanding the correct proportions of the face will help you accurately depict features, such as the eyes, nose, mouth, and ears.

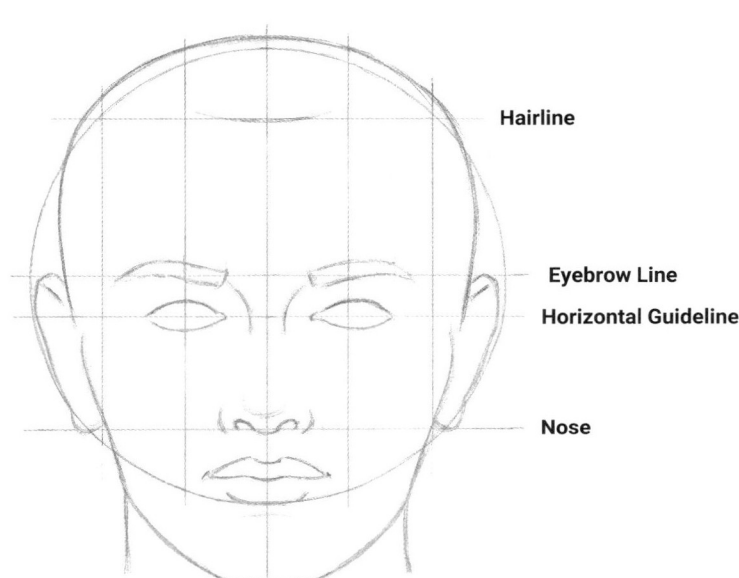

Vertical Guideline

Hairline

Eyebrow Line

Horizontal Guideline

Nose

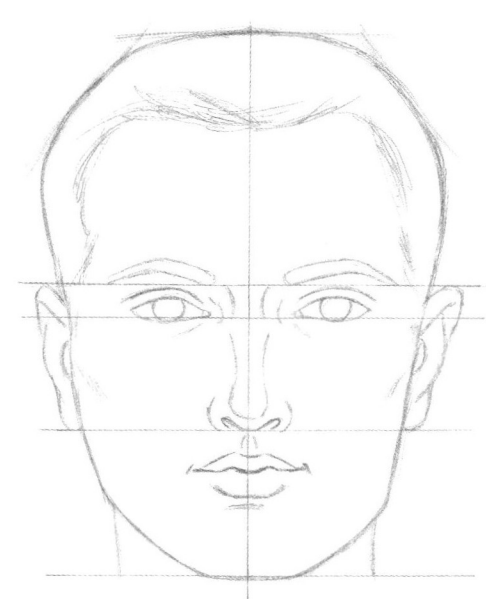

Guidelines The head resembles a ball that has been compressed at the sides. The ball is halved vertically and horizontally, and the face can be divided into three horizontal sections by the hairline, the eyebrow line, and the nose line. With these few guidelines, you can capture virtually any face.

Facial Features The eyes are positioned exactly between the horizontal line separating the eyebrows and the line of the brows. The tip of the nose is midway between the line of the brows and the chin. The lower lip ends midway between the nose and chin. The ears extend from the line of the brows to the level of the tip of the nose.

Practice filling in the facial features using the outline below.

Basic Eye Structure

Although eyes are such an important element of any portrait, they're surprisingly easy to draw—once you know how. Practice the construction until you're confident. Then you can take it a step further and learn how to build eyes freehand.

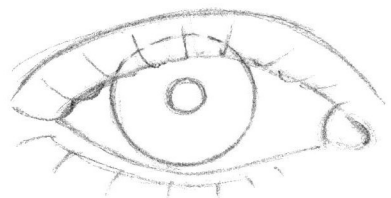

1 First, draw the circle for the iris; then place the crescent-shaped eyelid over it. Draw the lower eyelid, lashes, and the corner of the eye.

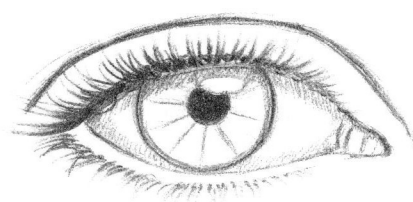

2 Now draw "rays" pointing outward from the pupil. Fill in the eyelashes and the upper eyelid, as well as the black pupil and the reflection of light.

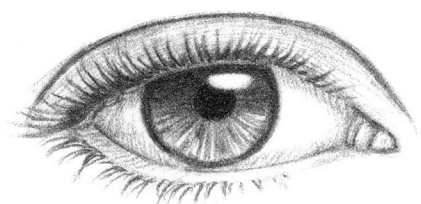

3 Add more color to the iris with radial strokes. Shape the upper and lower eyelids with hatching.

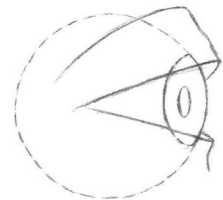

1 Draw a dashed circle, followed by the upper and lower eyelids. Viewed from the side, the iris and pupil are shaped like ellipses, each covered by the eyelid at the top and bottom.

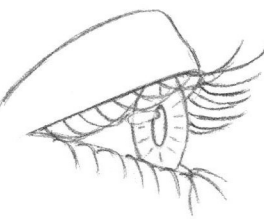

2 When viewed from the side, draw eyelashes from the inner to the outer corner of the eye. The eyelashes are longer above the center of the eye than on the sides.

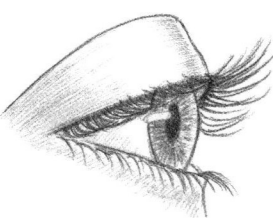

3 When shading the eyelids, work out from the semicircular shape.

Practice drawing eyes. Use photos for reference, if you like.

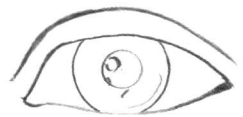

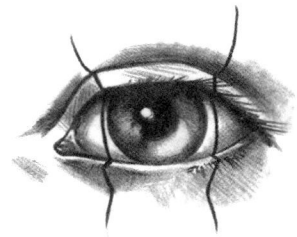

Nose and Lips

The nose and the lips are generally drawn together as a unit, but as you are learning, it's helpful to break them into parts. Noses come in all shapes and sizes. Start by dividing the nose into four distinct planes to indicate its shape. Don't forget to lift out highlights where the light source hits the nose, whether from the front or the side.

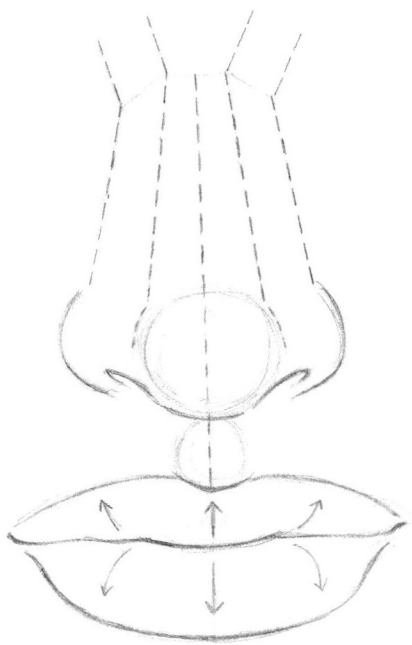 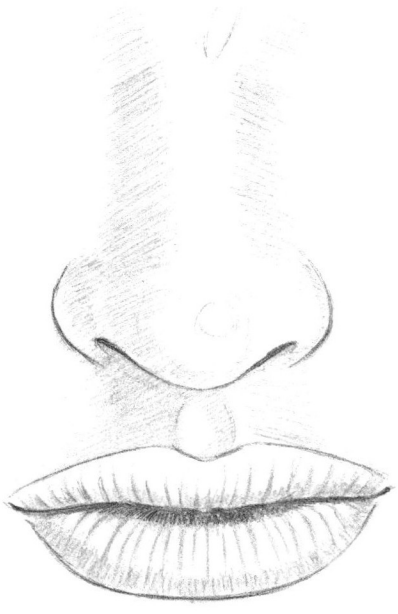 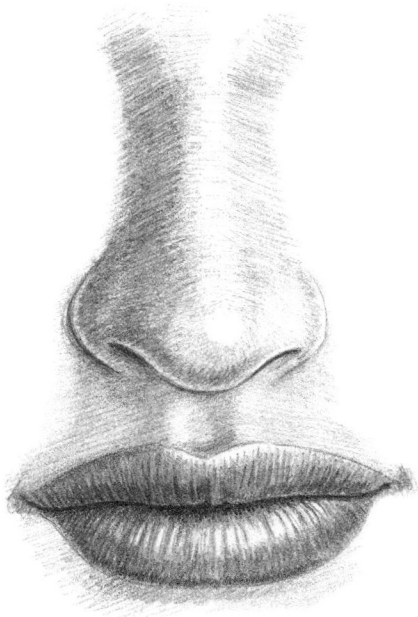

1 Indicate the nose with four planes and add a circle for the tip. Then draw the curves of the lips. The small circle between the upper lip and the nose indicates the hollow there. See the arrows on the upper and lower lips? You'll need to shade in this direction later.

2 Add hatching to the left and right of the nose, and then draw the nostrils. Indicate the hollow between the lip and nose. Hatch the lips in the direction of the arrows in step one, and draw the gap between the lips.

3 With the final shading, you'll give the nose and mouth their shape. Use a kneaded eraser to lift out highlights of varying brightness to the upper lip, the tip of the nose, and the bridge of the nose.

Practice drawing some noses here. Take your time and focus on getting comfortable with mastering your technique.

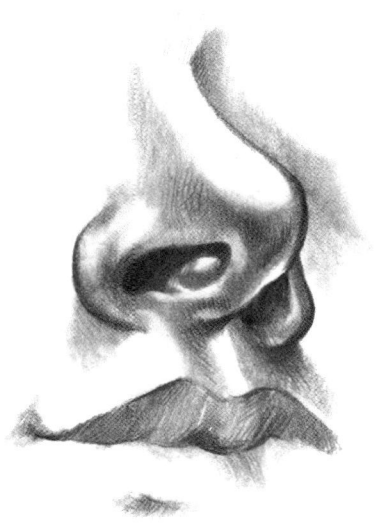

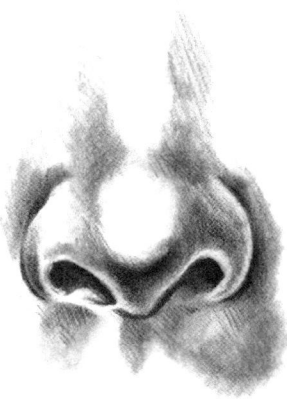

The Mouth

For beginners, it's easiest to draw lips in three steps. First, draw the basic shapes of the upper and lower lips, and then gradually add the shape of the mouth using curved lines and hatching. Draw your strokes so that they follow the natural curves of the mouth.

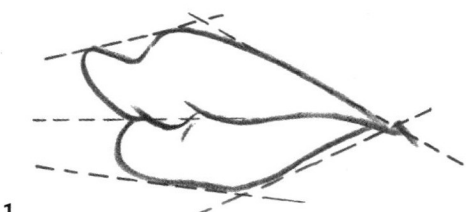

1

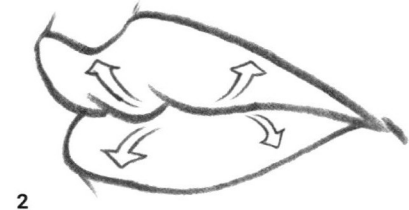

2

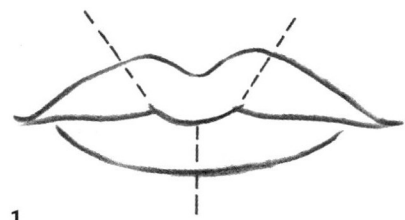

1

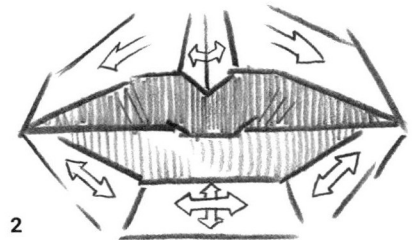

2

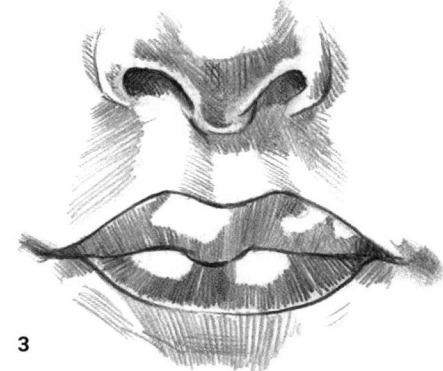

3

Start with a basic outline. Notice how the top lip slightly protrudes over the bottom lip. One lip might also be fuller than the other.

Begin shading in the direction of the lip planes. Shade the top lip using upward strokes; shade the bottom lip using downward strokes.

Use light hatching to create shading, leaving white to indicate highlights. If you shade too much, simply use a kneaded eraser to lift out the highlights.

Lips are easy to draw once you've had a little practice.
Try drawing lips here, including drawing some lips from a side view.

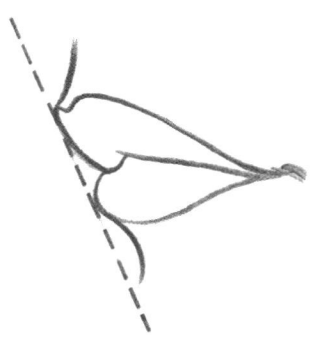

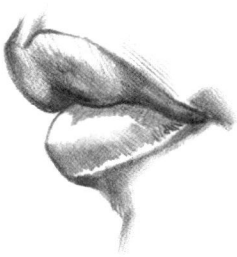

Establishing Values

Every skin tone is made up of a variety of values. When drawing in pencil, you can accurately capture these differing tones using varying degrees of light and shadow. Before you start drawing, be sure to study your subject to establish the richest darks and brightest lights.

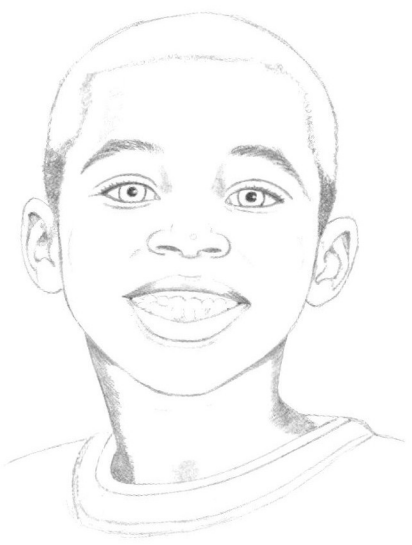

1 Start by sketching the outline of the head and face, placing the features. Using a 2B pencil, sketch in the neck and define the chin. Develop the eyes and use short, quick lines to draw the eyebrows.

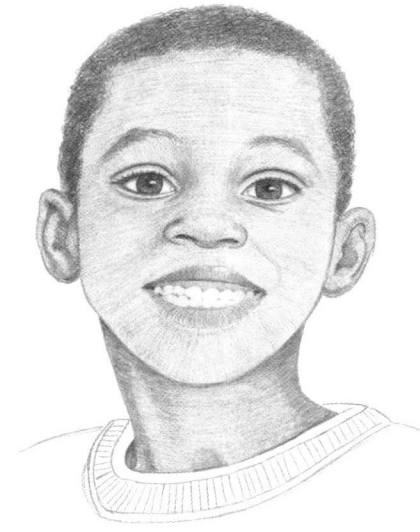

2 Shade the nose, neck, and top lip. Using quick, circular strokes, render the short, curly hair. Then detail the eyebrows and eyes.

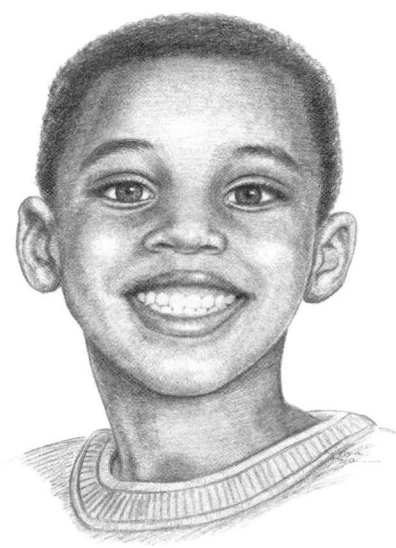

3 Apply a light layer of shading over the face, always varying the direction of strokes as necessary to follow the shapes of the different planes.

Practice establishing values using the outline below.
Remember to pay attention to the light source, so you can lift
out highlights where appropriate.

Drawing a Likeness

To capture a likeness in a portrait, study the unique features of your subject, such as the shape of their head and jawline; the details of their nose, lips, and eyes; and their hairline. The ability to draw a true likeness often rests on the seemingly little things.

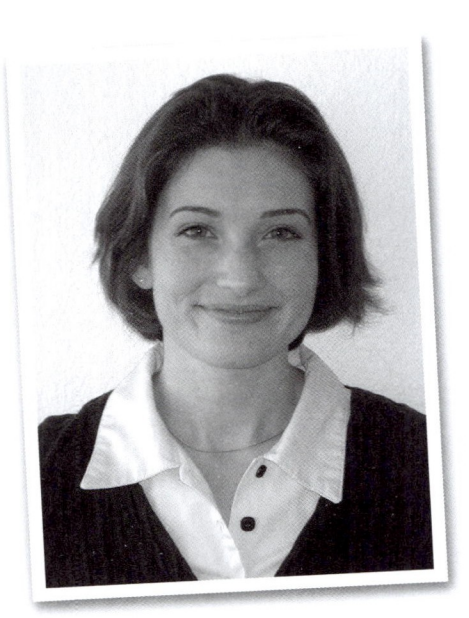

The photo showcases the delicate facial features, skin, and radiant eyes. Pay attention to individual characteristics, such as the slightly crooked mouth, laugh lines, and wide-set eyes. Noticing the details are crucial if you want to draw realistic portraits.

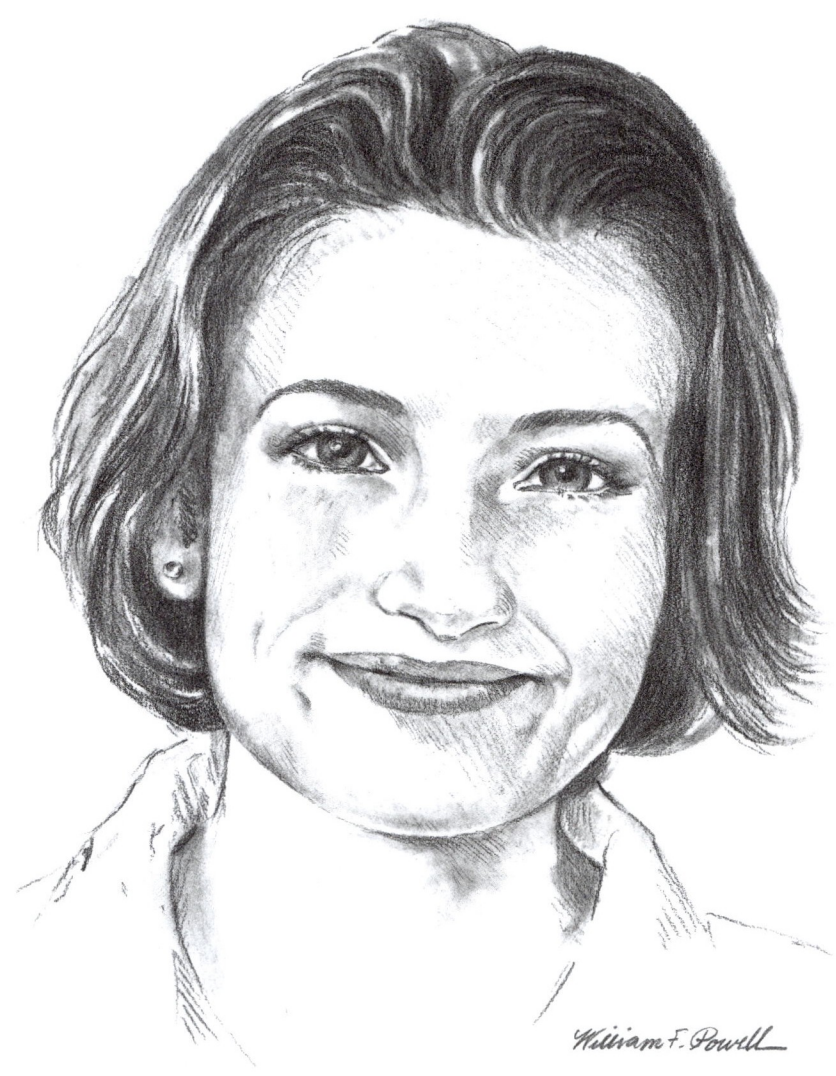

William F. Powell

Draw the iris and pupil as well as the laugh lines.
Refer to the photograph as needed to capture the finer details.

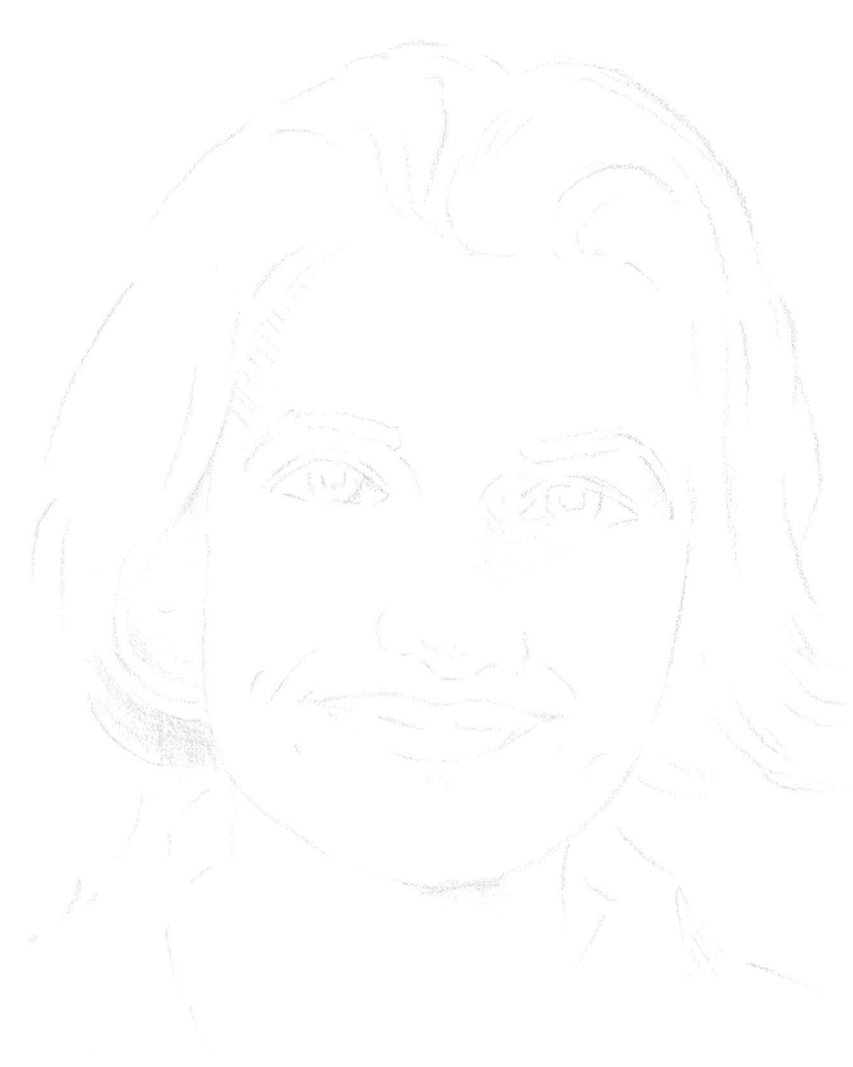

Drawing from Life

When drawing from a live model, you have an invaluable advantage: You can position the model in the light you like. When working outdoors, the model can change position until you're satisfied. In the studio, you can adjust the lighting until everything is just right.

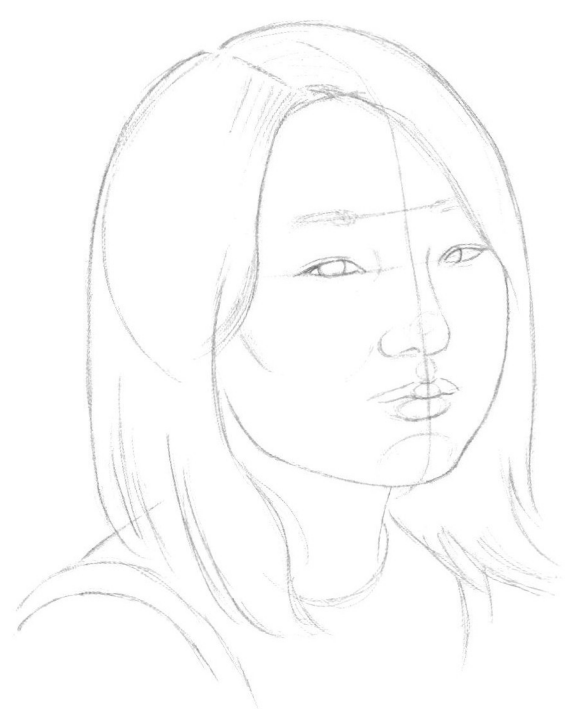

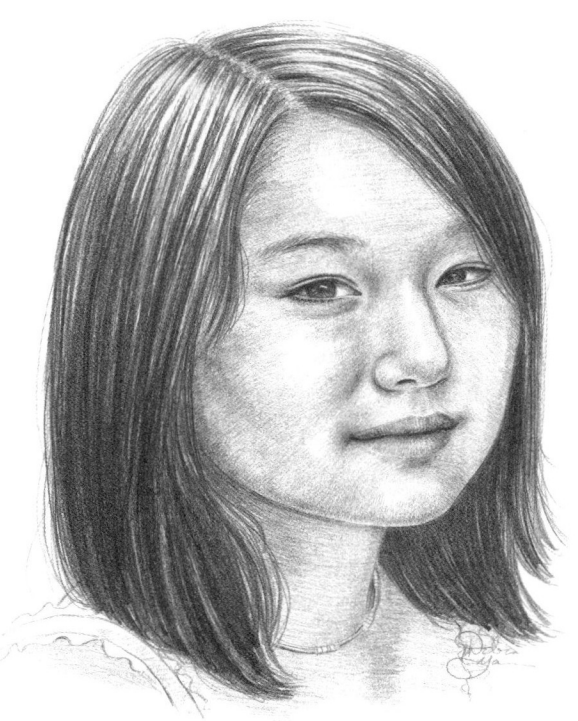

1 Block out the face in a three-quarter view, using broad shapes and light sketch lines. Note that one nostril is visible, and the mouth appears shorter on the left than on the right.

2 Using a 3B pencil, darken the hair. Then use a variety of shading techniques to add depth and form to the face. Use a kneaded eraser to lift out highlights or to soften pencil strokes.

Draw the hair with a 2H pencil, leaving plenty of white space
for the highlights. Use light horizontal strokes to suggest the shape
of the neck. Then add shading as needed.

Light and Shadow

Light is crucial to the atmosphere of a drawing. Shadows also depend on light, as they have more or less contrast depending on the lighting. A simple rule applies to the depiction of light in a portrait: Whatever is directly in the light is light and what is in shadow is dark.

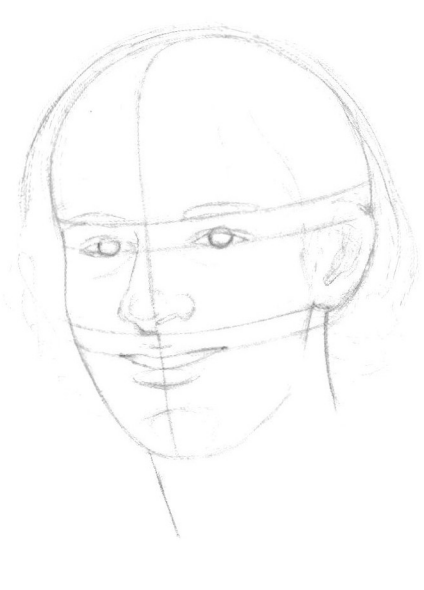 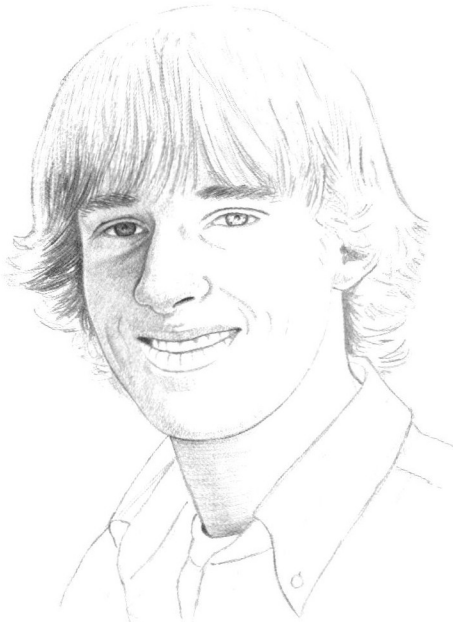 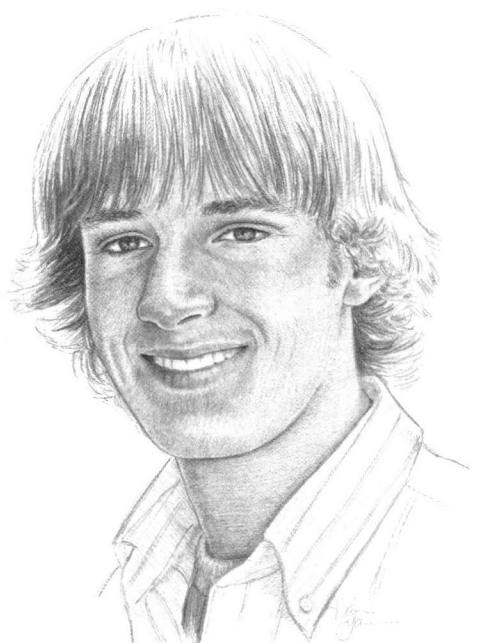

1 Using an HB pencil, outline the basic shapes of the head, neck, and hair. The boy's face is shown in a three-quarter view, so the centerline needs to be shifted to the left. Outline the facial features with light strokes—especially the rounded shape of the nose and chin.

2 Shade the left side of the face with a 2B pencil. Apply a fine layer of light, short strokes. Then, add lighter, longer strokes. Leave white in the hair to show where the light shines directly onto the subject. Blend the long strokes at the top of the head to make the hair look lifelike.

3 Using the 2B pencil, shade the face more finely—the right side remains significantly lighter than the left, as the light is coming from the right. Continue working on the eyes, neck, and shirt. Lift out highlights from the hair so it appears brightly illuminated.

Using an HB pencil, draw the initial details of the mouth, nose, eyes, and eyebrows. Shade in the dark areas with a 2B pencil. Finally, add fine shading for the face.

Capturing Details

For subjects with light hair, use subtle shading and just a few simple strokes. To indicate more fullness to a hairstyle, add darker shading around the ears and near the neck.

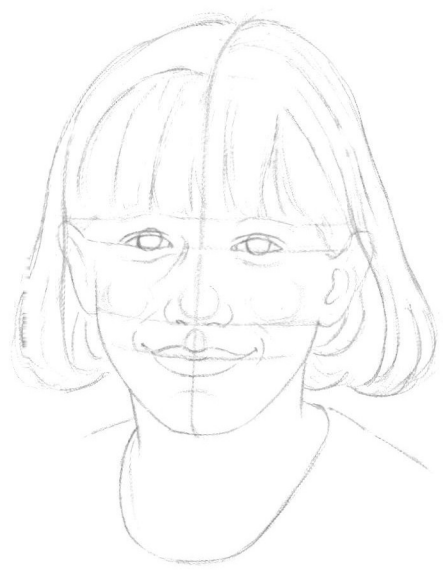

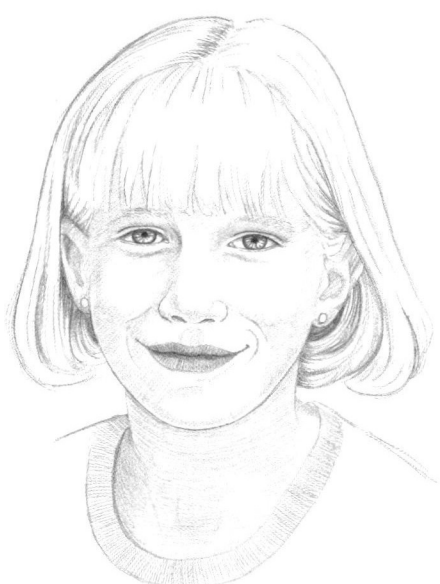

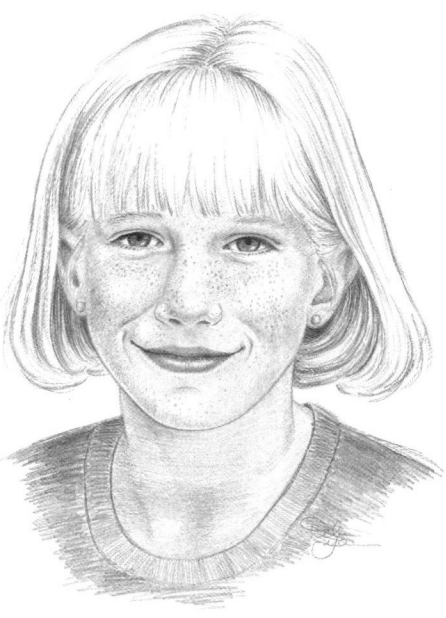

1 Using a 2B pencil, block out the facial features with guidelines, and begin to sketch in the details.

2 Shade the face with light, soft strokes, and make short, quick strokes for the eyebrows, keeping them light. Shade the irises using strokes that radiate out from the pupil. Add some hatching to the neckband of the shirt.

3 Using a kneaded eraser, pull out a highlight on the bottom lip. Then create more dark strands of hair and further develop the eyes and eyebrows. Add freckles, making sure that they vary in size and shape. To finish, shade the shirt using relatively dark strokes.

Continue working on the details of the face. Take your time with the hair, noting the darkest areas are next to the ear, where the hair is in shadow. Use a kneaded eraser to lift out highlights on the lower lip.

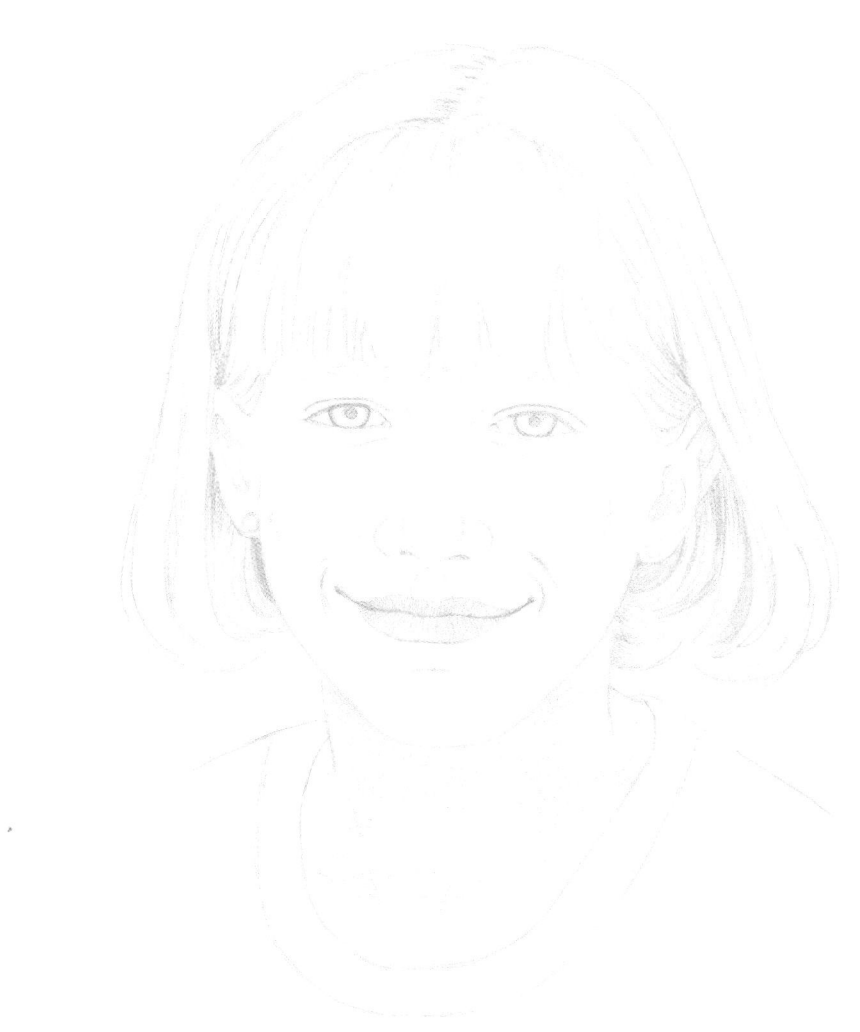

Toddler

To draw a realistic portrait of a toddler or small child, it's important to position the facial features correctly on the face and depict them in the correct size, appropriate to the subject's age. Also, keep in mind that the mouth and eyes are rounder than an adult's, and the hair is often fine and thin.

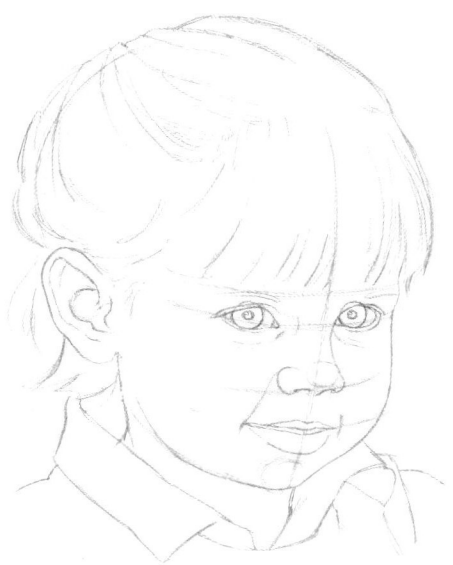

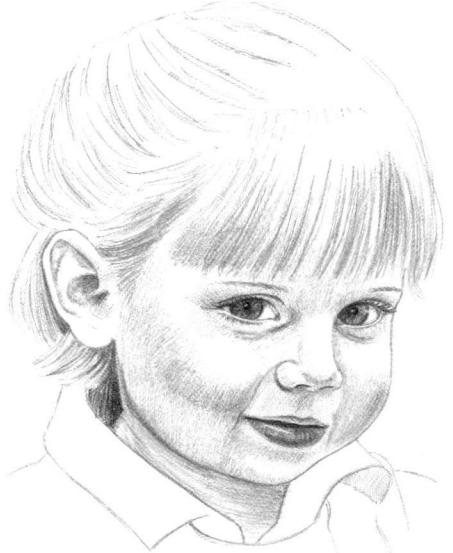

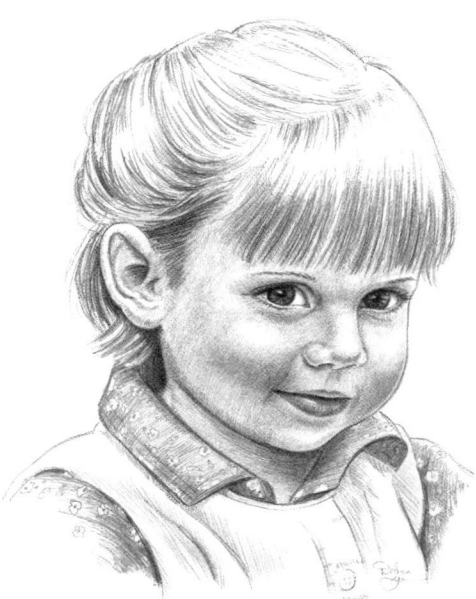

1 With a freshly sharpened pencil, draw the basic shape of the face. Draw the eyes in more detail, keeping in mind the light reflections—they give the eyes that curious, childlike expression.

2 Draw the eyelashes with curved strokes, and shape the crown of the head with soft up-and-down strokes. Soft hatching gives the right cheek its shape, and more soft strokes define the bangs.

3 Erase any white areas at the top of the fringe to depict the reflection of light. Use a 3B pencil to create the clothes. Now look at the portrait from a distance and check for any harsh transitions that detract from the overall impression of the little girl. Erase old lines.

Using a 3B pencil, draw the eyes, lips, and hair. Make sure to darken the hair between the crown and the ear. Use delicate, short strokes to give the hair a soft appearance. Use curved strokes to draw in the eyelashes.

Depicting Age

As we age, our skin's elasticity decreases: wrinkles appear, the nose and ears droop slightly, and lips become thinner. Consider these details when portraying an older person.

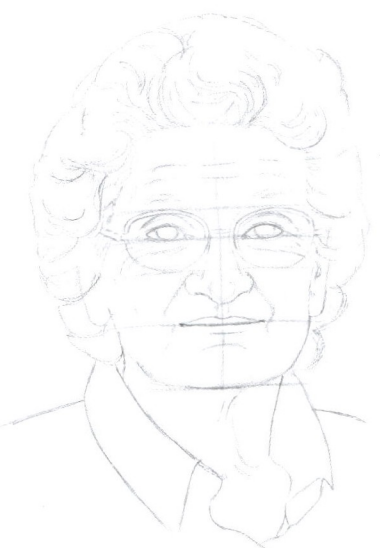

1 After determining the facial proportions and initial outlines, draw the contours of the glasses, the delicate lines around the eyes, and the wrinkles on the forehead. The chin and cheeks will be slightly wider and softer. Notice the wrinkles on the neck.

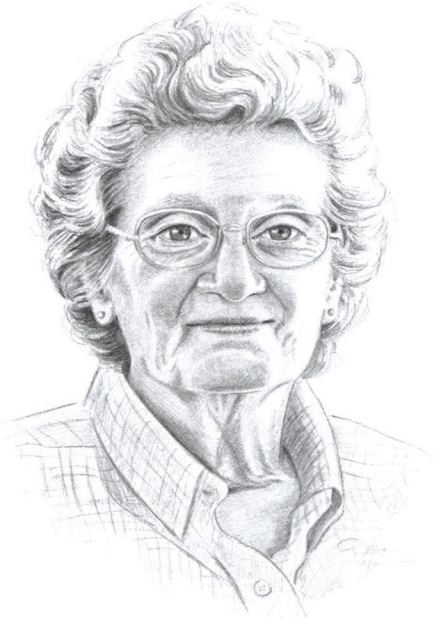

2 Shade the face in gray. Make sure to deepen the wrinkles around the eyes so they don't blend into the surface of the face. Smooth out any harsh transitions with a blending stump.

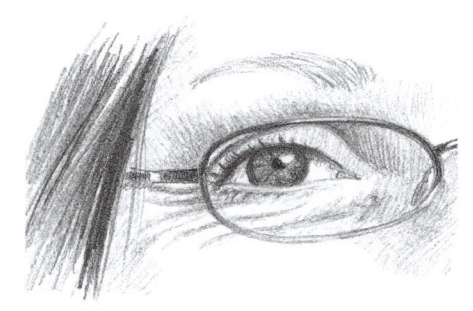

If you're drawing someone wearing glasses, enlarge the wrinkles behind the lenses. This is easy to achieve by slightly increasing the wrinkles and the distance between them.

Use a 2B pencil to develop the finer details of this subject, such as the wrinkles around the eyes, neck, and face. Pay attention to the hatching around the mouth and nose to create the impression of soft skin.

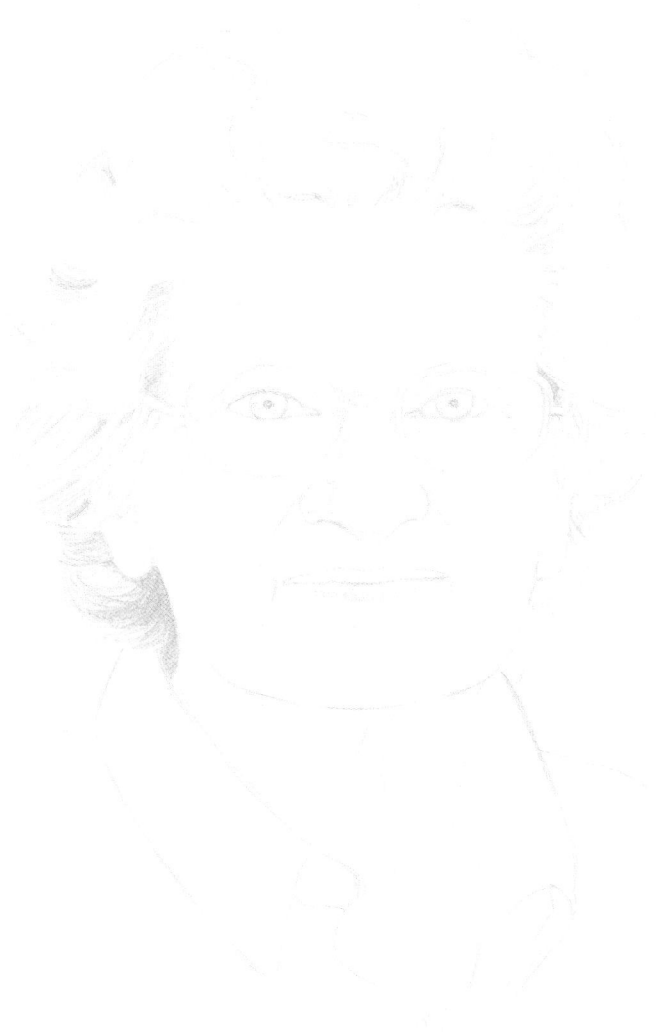

Hand Study

Hands and feet are not only highly expressive body parts, but also an artistic challenge. To familiarize yourself with the proportions of a hand, first draw three curved lines that are all the same distance apart. The fingertips all end on the outer line, the second joints on the second line, and the knuckles begin on the third line. The first finger joint is approximately halfway between the first and second lines. And the palm is the same length as the middle finger.

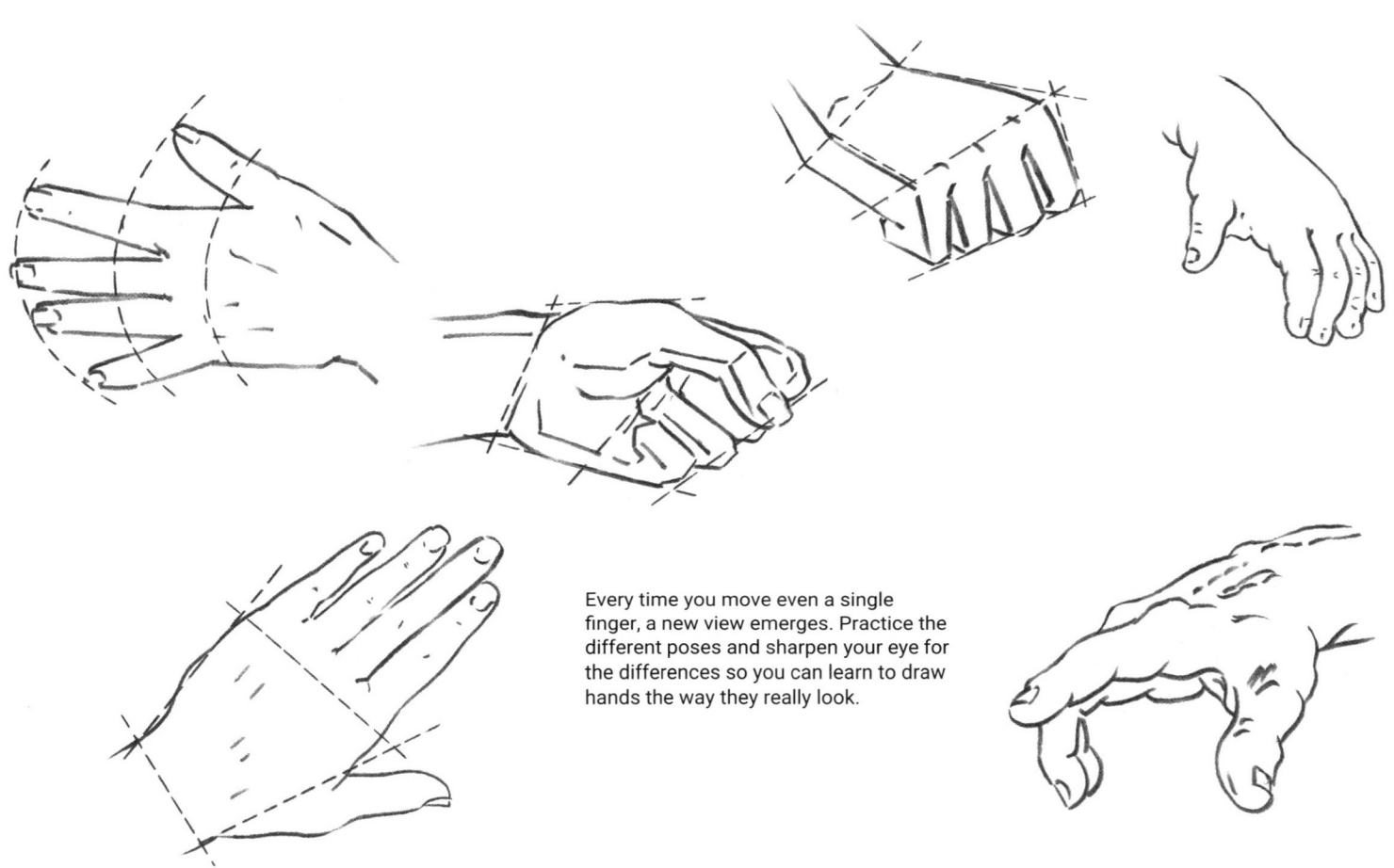

Every time you move even a single finger, a new view emerges. Practice the different poses and sharpen your eye for the differences so you can learn to draw hands the way they really look.

Your own hands are the best model. Draw your hand, or someone else's, moving in different positions. Observe the light and shadows!

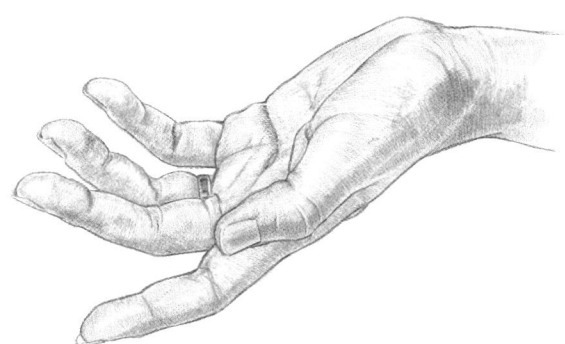

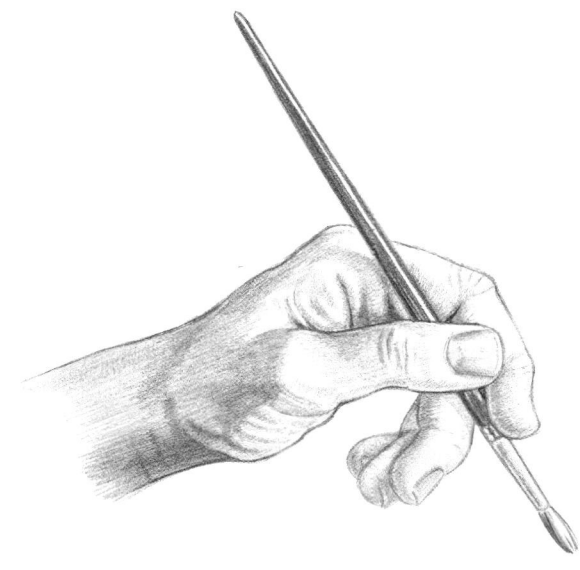

Body Proportions
of Children

To draw the little girl, start with a simple stick figure. Use circles, ovals, and rectangles to establish the general body shapes, and then develop the figure. Draw the outlines of the clothing.

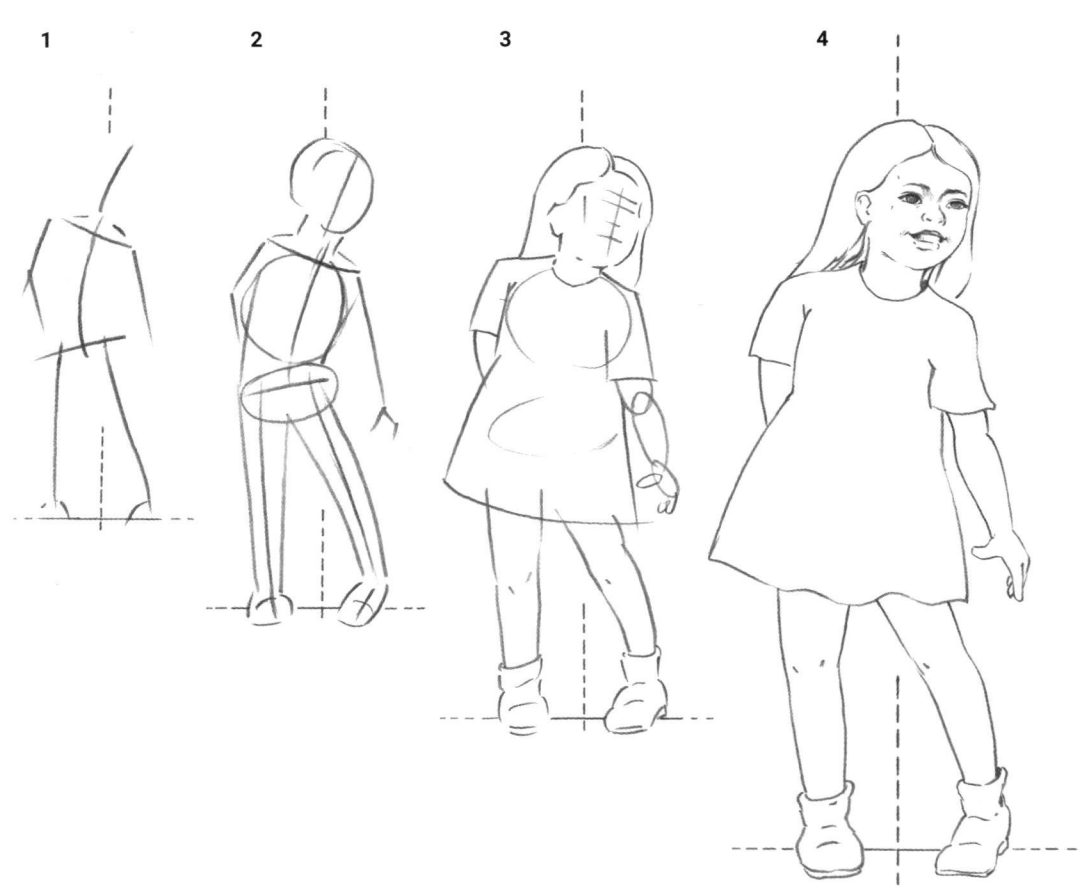

1   2   3   4

Practice drawing childlike proportions. Work on the more developed drawing first, focusing on the light and shadows around the face. Then use the stick figure to work on building the complete form.

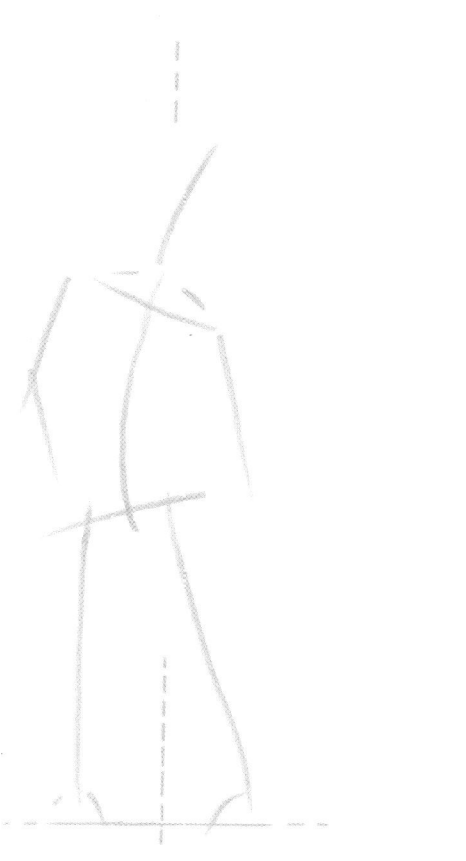

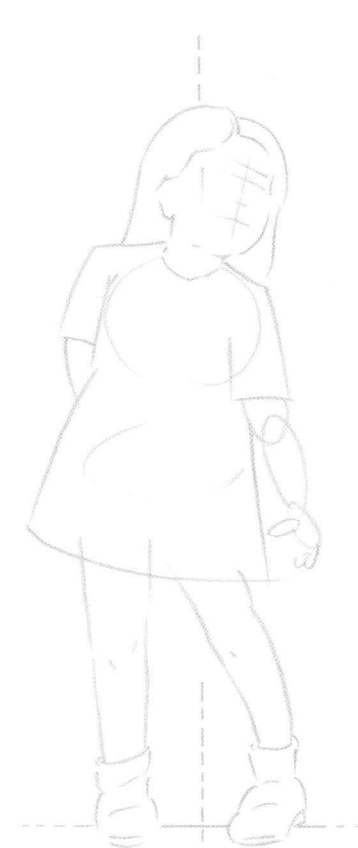

Quarto.com
WalterFoster.com

First published in 2026 by Walter Foster Publishing, an imprint of The Quarto Group,
100 Cummings Center, Suite 265-D, Beverly, MA 01915, USA.
T (978) 282-9590 F (978) 283-2742

EEA Representation, WTS Tax d.o.o.,
Žanova ulica 3, 4000 Kranj, Slovenia.
www.wts-tax.si

Walter Foster Publishing titles are also available at discount for retail, wholesale, promotional, and bulk purchase.
For details, contact the Special Sales Manager by email at specialsales@quarto.com or by mail at The Quarto
Group, Attn: Special Sales Manager, 100 Cummings Center, Suite 265-D, Beverly, MA 01915, USA.

30 29 28 27 26   1 2 3 4 5

ISBN: 978-1-57715-735-9

Digital edition published in 2026
eISBN: 978-1-57715-736-6

Produced by Coffee Cup Creative LLC
Layout by Debbie Aiken
Proofread by Stephanie Carbajal

Printed in Guangdong, China TT122025

Featured Artists

Michael Butkus · Walter T. Foster · Patricia Getha
Michele Maltseff · William F. Powell · Nolon Stacey
Mia Tavonatti · Linda Weil · Debra Kauffman Yaun